The Left Just Isn't Right

The Left Just Isn't Right

David Limbaugh

Creators Publishing
Hermosa Beach, CA

The Left Just Isn't Right
Copyright © 2018 Creators Publishing

Cover art by Peter Kaminski

CREATORS PUBLISHING
737 3rd St
Hermosa Beach, CA 90254
310-337-7003

ISBN (print): 978-1-945630-85-9
ISBN (ebook): 978-1-945630-84-2

First Edition
Printed in the United States of America
1 3 5 7 9 10 8 6 4 2

A Note From the Publisher

Since 1987, Creators has syndicated many of your favorite columns to newspapers. In this digital age, we are bringing collections of those columns to your fingertips. This will allow you to read and reread your favorite columnists, with your own personal digital archive of their work.

Creators Publishing

Contents

Petty Partisanship From an Exiting Obama

January 6, 2017

I don't know about you, but I feel a strong sense of optimism in the air. However, neither President Obama nor his Democratic Party shares it, and the Democrats are gearing up for obstruction mode — not a renewed period of cooperation, which they always demand when they're in power.

American businesses are relieved that President Obama's anti-business boot will finally be lifted from their throats. They are energized by President-elect Donald Trump's promises to reduce their tax and regulatory burden and re-establish a pro-entrepreneurial climate.

We are already seeing concrete results. Ford announced that it is canceling its plans to invest $1.3 billion in a new manufacturing plant in Mexico and will instead devote $700 million to expand production in the United States. CEO Mark Fields said: "We look at all factors, including what we view as a more positive U.S. manufacturing business environment under President-elect Trump. And it's literally a vote of confidence around some of the pro-growth policies that he has been outlining, and that's why we're making this decision to invest here in the U.S."

Another positive sign comes from economists at HSBC Bank, who raised their forecast for global growth over the next two years based on robust manufacturing activity, a resilient China and, most of all, the fiscal boost expected to come in the United States.

President Obama has falsely claimed that the U.S. economy under his watch has been robust, but everyone knows better, and these optimistic signs we're witnessing in anticipation of the Trump presidency are proof of it.

But Obama and the Democrats will have none of it. They are not about to stand by while people criticize Obama's poor economic record. They must perpetuate the fiction that his leftist policies worked, so the propaganda continues.

After every presidential election in which their candidate wins, Democrats claim a strong mandate to advance their agenda and shame Republicans for resisting. When Republican George W. Bush won a narrow victory over Democrat Al Gore in 2000, they spent most of their time trying to delegitimize Bush — falsely charging that he had stolen the election, which they had actually tried to steal themselves.

Trump won an impressive electoral victory in November, but Democrats have nevertheless denied he has any mandate at all, citing his loss in the popular vote and claiming Russian hacking helped him win. Both of these claims are bogus. Our presidents are elected by the Electoral College, not by the total popular vote, and under our system, Trump has a strong mandate. Not only was Trump's electoral victory decisive but also a shocking percentage of counties supported Trump, and the Republicans' level of control of state governments is staggering.

Democrats have signaled they are going to obstruct Trump's agenda from the get-go. What do you expect when their hero is in full-on Trump-sabotage mode on his way out of the Oval Office?

Democrats have already taken aim at Trump's proposed nominees, as opposed to the GOP's rapid approval of Obama's Cabinet appointees. Senate Minority Leader Chuck Schumer said Democrats will work with Trump only if he "moves completely in (the Democrats') direction and abandons his Republican colleagues." Can you imagine the outcry if Republicans had made such a statement toward Obama in 2008?

But Obama himself is leading the charge. The Hill reports that "Obama has taken a number of unilateral actions in the waning days of his tenure that appear designed to box in President-elect Donald Trump." The Hill, no liberal rag, is exactly right. Examples abound:

his ban on oil and gas drilling across large swaths of the Atlantic and Arctic oceans, his closing off of 1.6 million acres of Western land to development, his eliminating a registration system used mostly on Muslim immigrants, his administration's abstention on the United Nations Security Council vote condemning Israeli settlements and Secretary of State John Kerry's subsequent speech maligning Israel on this issue, and Obama's sanctioning of Russian entities for allegedly influencing our presidential election. Obama is also planning to move ahead with his reckless plan to release more prisoners from Guantanamo Bay despite Trump's urging a halt to the process. And Obama made a trip to Capitol Hill to embolden Democrats to resist any GOP efforts to repeal Obamacare. The "bipartisan" exemplar met only with Democrats, urging them not to "rescue" Republicans by helping them to pass Obamacare replacement measures.

How can we not see the vindictiveness behind Obama's actions? He is now sanctioning Russia when, according to Sen. Tom Cotton, he actively blocked measures to take a firmer line on Russia during his term and when, according to former U.S. Ambassador to the United Nations John Bolton, he allowed the Russians to walk all over him for eight years.

On top of all this, Obama petulantly claimed that he could have won a third term if he had been permitted to run against Trump. He is just beside himself that the American electorate so resoundingly rejected his agenda. Obama also said that Hillary Clinton would have won in a landslide if young people had been the only ones who voted.

This is nothing but pure class from the man who promised to bring hope and change and a renewed spirit of bipartisanship to America.

Liberals Are Putting Conservatism, Not Just Sen. Sessions, on Trial

January 13, 2017

The Senate confirmation hearings for Sen. Jeff Sessions' attorney general nomination show that the liberal establishment learned nothing from the 2016 elections and will continue to wage war on conservatives as if they were enemies of the republic — and humanity.

Democratic attacks on Sessions are not grounded in any concern that he is a racist or has something terrible in his ancient history. They know that Sessions is not a racist and that he is an honorable man. His disqualifying sin, in their eyes, is that he is a conservative — and a Southern one at that, which makes it even easier to demonize him as a bigot.

For if you watched the hearings, you saw that it was not Sessions particularly who was on trial but conservatism and all subscribing to it.

Nor is the rule of law a genuine concern to Democrats, despite their gnashing of teeth over faux fears that Sessions would refuse to enforce certain progressive laws already on the books. They only care about the rule of law when invoking it benefits them politically. In fact, one of the main reasons they oppose Sessions is that he indeed is committed to the rule of law and the impartial administration of justice. They are agenda-oriented above all and willfully trample the rule of law when it interferes with their progressive ends.

When Republicans grill liberal nominees for judicial and executive positions, which is rare, they don't badger them over their political views. They don't shame them for the crime of being liberal. They press them on whether they would honor the Constitution and the rule of law and whether they would act within the legal constraints of their positions. But Democratic interrogation of Republican nominees invariably descends into a shaming of the nominee for his political beliefs — or for his votes on measures they disagree with, even when the votes are for measures that are unarguably constitutional.

The liberal establishment in the Democratic Party and in the liberal media (and Hollywood and academia) simply cannot grasp that half the country is conservative. In fact, 11 percent more Americans identify as conservatives than as liberals.

It never occurs to most of these leftist movers and shakers that conservatives have noble and justifiable reasons for their views. They oppose Obamacare not because they have no compassion for the poor and downtrodden but because it is destroying everything in its path — because it raises rates and reduces quality of care and medical choices. They don't oppose radical, reckless and economically smothering environmental policies because they don't care about clean air and water, because they place their selfish financial interests above the health and welfare of Americans or because they are science deniers. They reject the presumptuous, dishonest and extreme conclusions of a make-believe, highly politicized scientific consensus, and they know that the left's proposed draconian measures wouldn't materially alleviate the problems even if they exist and are man-made as the left speciously contends. They oppose the flooding of our borders with immigrants who aren't coming legally and the admission of insufficiently vetted potential terrorists not because they are bigoted toward Muslims or uncompassionate for people but because they believe in preserving the American idea and in protecting American citizens. They oppose confiscatory taxes and continued escalations of the national debt not because they are sinister engineers of ever greater income inequality (which liberal policies actually exacerbate) but because these things cripple the nation's economic engines and reduce prosperity across the board. They are not opponents but champions of voting rights because they demand that people who vote be actually legally entitled to vote. They oppose abortion not because they disrespect and undervalue women but because they value all human life, especially the most innocent. They support a strong military not because they are imperialists and want to impose American will throughout the planet but because they believe American strength is conducive to peace. The same analysis applies to almost any political issue. Conservatives' views are prudential and morally sound.

But listen to Meryl Streep — both the content of her patronizing remarks and her condescending tone. Listen to Sen. Pat Leahy, Sen. Cory Booker and their fellow Democrats castigating Sessions for his reasonable votes on issues that happen to interfere with the sacred liberal agenda.

Americans — at least half of us — are tired of being maligned by the left as evil, stupid and bigoted because we won't fall in lockstep with this agenda.

One might think that after eight years of failed liberal policies, Democrats would be more inclined to eat crow than to lecture the rest of America for rejecting their manifestly destructive policy prescriptions. If so, one would be wrong and wholly ignorant of the liberal worldview and mindset.

It's bad enough that liberals can never accept accountability for their failures, but it is really unbearable to listen to their highhanded, misguided lectures. They lost for a reason, but they'll never stop fighting and trying to shame the rest of us, so kudos to President-elect Donald Trump for giving it back to them even better than they are dishing it out. How refreshing. Finally!

Obama's Inexcusable Commutation
January 20, 2017

I highly doubt that President Obama commuted Chelsea Manning's sentence out of compassion — and suspect it was just one more slap in America's face on his way out the door.

Out of all the possible beneficiaries of his presidential pardon pen, why would Obama single out this unrepentant traitor for leniency? Well, Manning was convicted of espionage as Bradley Manning. I suppose Manning's gender transformation could have played a part in Obama's mind, as those types of leftist causes always seem to trump other concerns, such as national security.

What possible mitigating facts could move a person of ordinary sensibilities and a healthy respect for our armed services, our national defense and the rule of law to ignore the mountains of incriminating and aggravating evidence and substitute his judgment for the military trial judge's?

Well, the political left is always looking for a good whistleblower — unless he or she is exposing the misdeeds of a leftist administration, such as the unrewarded witnesses against the government in the Operation Fast and Furious fiasco. When the informant can embarrass the U.S. military — that takes the cake.

Among the hundreds of thousands of classified documents that Manning stole with the specific intention of delivering them to WikiLeaks for public dissemination was a video of American soldiers in Iraq involved in a very problematic and possibly illegal shooting.

But if exposing this video was Manning's burning motive, why didn't she solely release it and not the truckloads of other sensitive materials?

Even if we were inclined to sympathize with Manning's gender confusion (though I thought the left would never consider gender transformation as anything other than triumphant liberation), would it be worth it to send a signal diminishing the gravity of this offense and the harm and potential harm it caused?

The military judge had before her all exculpatory evidence when she rendered her decision and sentenced Manning. She could have sentenced Manning to 136 years but chose 35 years instead, which suggests she weighed all the positive and negative factors. Moreover, Secretary of Defense Ash Carter and the Pentagon opposed President Obama's actions.

Understand that Manning pleaded guilty to the charges, and they were based on a shocking immensity of damning evidence. Manning was a private first class deployed on foreign soil from November 2009 to May 2010 and had access to top-secret information. During that time, she downloaded some 400,000 classified files concerning the Iraq War, more than 90,000 from the war in Afghanistan, a quarter-million diplomatic emails, classified videos of U.S. airstrikes and classified files from the prison in Guantanamo Bay. (This last one probably earned her bonus points from Obama.)

Does this sound like someone who wanted to expose an isolated incident of alleged wrongdoing or someone who was deeply committed to harming the United States, compromising fellow soldiers, endangering Americans throughout the world and aiding and abetting the causes of terrorists and other enemies of the United States?

What were the consequences of this betrayal? It sent the State Department into crisis and caused great expenditures of time and money to assess the damage from the leaks. Fox News reports that ambassadors were forced to resign and CIA station chiefs were recalled. And according to Defense Department officials, Manning's treachery accelerated the Arab Spring and possibly contributed to the rise of the Islamic State group. Further, two intelligence sources confirmed that after the release of two Afghanistan reports in 2010, the Taliban reportedly went on a killing spree and took out everyone fitting the description of those working with the United States. These sources said there is no question that the Taliban killed people after the leaks and that this had a chilling effect on subsequent recruiting.

Where are liberals on all this? They were apoplectic over Russian attempts to interfere with our election but are immovably indifferent to national security leaks that compromise the interests of the United States and benefit Russia and other foreign governments. Let's please not indulge the fiction that their interest in the Russian interference allegations is anything other than an opportunity to delegitimize Donald Trump's election and his presidency.

Obama has continually shown us where his sympathies lie. Even usually mild-mannered Paul Ryan said this commutation is outrageous and sets a "dangerous precedent" that those guilty of compromising our national security will not have to pay for their crimes.

Obama is also sending a signal that protecting our troops and other personnel who devote their lives to defending the nation and keeping Americans safe is a low priority — that safeguarding our national security interests and secrets is just not that big of a deal.

Sen. John McCain called the commutation a "grave mistake" that could encourage more espionage and undermine whistleblowers who operate through the proper channels. With all due respect to Sen. McCain, this was no mistake. It was a deliberate action by President Obama through which he once again communicated his disrespect, if not outright contempt, for the greatest military on the face of the earth, which was under his charge, regrettably, for the past eight years.

Pot-Kettle Media Call Trump Insecure

January 27, 2017

The Associated Press reports that President Donald Trump is "dogged by insecurity over his loss of the popular vote" and over "media coverage," but I have a different idea about whose insecurity is on display.

The entire liberal establishment and rank-and-file leftists remain in denial over Trump's victory. They convinced themselves from the beginning that Trump was a joke who stood no chance of winning the Republican primary, much less the general election.

They were so sure he couldn't beat Hillary Clinton that they went easy on him during the primaries, though Republicans knew their calculated restraint would have a short shelf life. Sure enough, during the general election campaign, they unloaded on him daily, yet they remained certain he could never win. They all but called the election at 5 p.m. on election night. For them, it has been downhill ever since.

The media elite, Democratic politicians and leftist constituencies are more unhinged now than they were when George W. Bush beat Al Gore in 2000 — and that is a mouthful. After the election, they worked themselves into a frenzy over Trump's agenda, which they now had to actually worry about, and what they perceived as his authoritarian tendencies, even comparing him to Adolf Hitler.

Of course, they also used Nazi analogies to malign Bush, but those were mostly strategic. Some of them really fear that Trump will declare martial law or unilaterally decree a moratorium on women's freedoms — loosely defined.

What's funny is that they never once feared, much less complained about, President Barack Obama's lawless authoritarianism, because he used it to advance an agenda they supported. They were tickled pink when he implemented provisions of the DREAM Act by executive order after lamenting just weeks earlier that he didn't have the authority to do it because Congress had explicitly rejected the measure. They had no problem with his selective exemptions under Obamacare, and they were indifferent to his rank politicization of the Justice Department and the IRS' targeting of conservatives.

Given leftists' propensity for projection, it is not surprising that they now suspect that Trump will be as highhanded as Obama — but to further a conservative agenda instead of their sacred liberal one. Now they will suddenly start caring about the Constitution again — though there is nothing unconstitutional in using the presidential pen to repeal unlawful executive orders.

Trump's sensitivity is hardly the issue here. Have you ever seen the media pre-emptively attack an incoming Democratic president? Have you ever seen the White House press pool interrogate a Democratic presidential press spokesman and ask him whether he intends to be truthful? The liberal media's antagonism to Trump is palpable.

In their article, the AP's Julie Pace and Jonathan Lemire characterize as "false" Trump's claim that he lost the popular vote because 3 million to 5 million people illegally cast ballots. I admit that I have no idea what level of voter fraud exists in this country, but observing the Democrats' behavior in Florida alone during the 2000 presidential election proves there's a problem. When you also consider the Democrats' specious opposition to voter ID laws, their defense of voter intimidation tactics and their long history of paying people to vote, you have reasonable grounds for suspicion, not to mention the credible research of John Fund and others documenting that there is indeed cause for concern.

But the media would never depict even an objectively provable lie of Obama's as false or challenge his presidential spokesman on it. Just look at the many tales they spun about Obamacare, unemployment, the deficit, the Islamic State group and a host of other issues. Even if turns out that Trump is dead wrong on his claim, the media now cannot fairly say it is false when there has yet to be an investigation. They don't know; I don't know; you don't know.

It is refreshing to me and millions of others that Trump directly responds to the left's shameless, deceitful efforts to undermine his legitimacy. The bullying, dishonest liberal establishment needs to be pushed back, and no one in my lifetime has shown himself to be more effective at doing it, with the possible exception of Ronald Reagan.

Whether or not Trump is too sensitive to liberals' efforts to delegitimize him, they are in fact trying, in bad faith, to do so, and they are failing. The more they pile on, the bigger a hole they will dig for themselves.

While they are rejoicing over Trump's supposed distraction from substantive issues, he is boldly, quickly and decisively advancing his agenda, putting the lie to their claims and leaving them stunned. They don't know what it's like be on the receiving end of an aggressive, action-oriented leader who, despite their claims, is not deterred by their organized caterwauling.

No, it is not Trump who is on the ropes here, and he is anything but distracted. He obviously is adroit at juggling many balls at the same time and staying focused on his campaign promises.

It's too early to tell how effective Trump will be in office — obviously — but he is off to a good start. I confess I am still somewhat concerned about his trade policies, but finally we have someone in office who appears to be unafraid to take action and who is not preoccupied with trying to appease the implacable liberal establishment.

With his business and leadership skills and his impatience for bureaucratic and Beltway inertia, Trump could make a significant positive difference in this country — and more quickly than we've been accustomed to expect from Republican politicians.

Let the media continue to bellyache and point the finger at Trump for being distracted, because with all their sound and fury, they are discrediting and emasculating themselves. Full speed ahead.

Let's Hope the Loony Left
Keeps Exposing Itself

February 3, 2017

How deliciously ironic that the unhinged Democrats are fueling, not paralyzing, President Donald Trump and energizing, not intimidating, his supporters — whose numbers are growing.

The entire liberal establishment — from the cultural crybabies to the lefty campus snowflakes to the mainstream media to the leading Democratic politicians — is having a nervous breakdown, and it is ugly and self-defeating.

These bullies have been doing for years what they're now falsely accusing Trump and the Republicans of doing. They are the ones who try to suppress speech, who act lawlessly and tyrannically, who undermine the democratic process, who breach the peace and who disrupt our domestic tranquility.

I remember talking to some college students in liberal la-la land after the election who were swallowing the liberals' scaremongering narrative that America was on the verge of becoming a police state. They really thought Trump might impose martial law, that he would suppress women's rights, that he would discriminate against minorities, that he would cause the stock market to crash immediately and that he would start a nuclear war.

I told them they had nothing to fear from Trump regarding any of that and that this was all manufactured madness from liberals who were merely projecting. If they wanted to be vigilant against any group, I said, they ought to watch the left, which was just getting warmed up for a four-year sustained temper tantrum.

It's just a beautifully simplistic plan. The left goes ballistic over Trump's election, warning of impending doom. No sooner has he been sworn in than they try to fulfill their own prophecy by staging phony protests about the horrors Trump is supposedly already visiting on the nation. They lied in their prophecy, and they are lying to create the false appearance that their warnings have been validated. They are behaving like petulant children, unwilling even to accept the legitimacy of the election, much less give Trump a chance to prove them wrong.

Their conduct — across the board — is inexcusable. Just consider their outrages so far — and notice how they are guilty of precisely the behavior they are condemning:

—The Women's March on Washington was ostensibly to protest Trump's vulgarity and policy noxiousness, but it actually pitted women against men, celebrated and glorified the killing of innocent unborn children, and provided a forum for morally and mentally disturbed celebrities, such as Madonna, to utter their own vulgarities and thoughts of violent acts (e.g., blowing up the White House). Do these people ever consider the embarrassing hypocrisy of their promoting and committing violence in the name of protesting violence from the right, as paranoid and unwarranted as their fear of such violence is?

—There were violent protests over a planned speech by Breitbart editor Milo Yiannopoulos at the University of California, Berkeley. The students' rationale? Yiannopoulos' message — which ridicules and condemns leftist duplicity, especially on free speech — incites violence. But the only violence it incites comes from them.

—Acting Attorney General Sally Yates showed audacity and impropriety in refusing to enforce a legal order of the president's designed to protect American citizens. What would the left have done if a Republican holdover had dared to defy an Obama order? What would the liberal media's response have been?

—Militant loony Sarah Silverman, during the Berkeley riots, tweeted, in effect, that the military should overthrow President Trump. Not to be outdone, her fellow Hollywood liberal Judd Apatow tweeted in reference to the Berkeley riots, "This is just the beginning. When will all the fools who are still supporting Trump realize what is at stake?"

—A woman interrupted the confirmation vote of the Senate Judiciary Committee on the nominee for attorney general, Jeff Sessions, with this outburst: "You have furthered the nomination of a man who will not protect the vulnerable."

—House Minority Leader Nancy Pelosi says Trump's Supreme Court justice nominee, Neil Gorsuch, has hostility toward children in school and children with autism. "It's a very hostile appointment," Pelosi told CNN's Jake Tapper. "Hail fellow well met, lovely family, I'm sure, but as far as your family is concerned — and if you breathe air, drink water, eat food, take medicine or in any other way interact with the courts — this is a very bad decision."

—Democratic Sen. Elizabeth Warren says Gorsuch is the reward to powerful interests who have tried "to turn the Supreme Court into one more rigged game that works only for the rich and the powerful." This is the thanks Gorsuch gets for his commitment to honoring the Constitution and the rule of law instead of imposing an ideological agenda.

These are but a few of the myriad examples of unhinged liberals who are living in — and trying to spread — their false reality. Law-abiding citizens, however, have nothing to fear from these people because their actions are backfiring. Their goal is to demonize, delegitimize and emasculate President Trump, Republicans and conservatives, but they are making them stronger and more popular.

The crazier these liberals become the more people will realize just who represents a threat in America — and it's not Trump and the Republicans. Primarily because of Trump's refreshing and bold actions so far — but also because of liberal irrationality and bad faith — even formerly tentative and squishy Republicans are getting behind Trump to advance a long-overdue remedial agenda to restore America's greatness.

I hope liberals keep it up — showing every day exactly who they are and how out of the mainstream they are — because it will further marginalize them and facilitate the advance of pro-growth and pro-security conservative policies.

The Story of Reality

February 10, 2017

Greg Koukl's "The Story of Reality" is one of the most important books I've read in a long time, and I want to encourage you — Christians and non-Christians — to read it. I know of no more efficient way to introduce you to the meaning of Christianity and the Christian worldview.

Sometimes even Christians reduce the Gospel message to its simplest form and talk as though the Bible began with the New Testament. But the Gospel didn't arise in a vacuum.

When Jesus died to save sinners, he did so in the context of a divinely orchestrated storyline of human history. As Nancy Pearcey observes in her compelling foreword to the book, "Christianity cannot be reduced to a tract or a technique for getting 'saved.' It is a comprehensive account of the structure of reality, a rational and real-world account of the history of the universe, a verifiable storyline of the unfolding of the cosmos."

Though Jesus delivered the most sublime moral teachings known to man, Koukl insists that "the two indispensable things you need to know about Jesus have little to do with his teachings in general. Instead they have to do with who Jesus was and what he came to accomplish, also known as the person and the work of Christ."

And this is critical: "The divide for Jesus was not between the poor and the rich, but between the proud and the repentant, regardless of income or social standing. Miss that, and you miss everything," writes Koukl. "These are the facts we must face if we are to get Jesus right. 'Social justice' is not the Gospel. It was not Jesus' message. It was not why he came. His real message was much more radical. Jesus' teaching — and the Story itself — focuses on something else. Not on the works of *Christians* but rather on the work of *Christ*. That is what the Story teaches."

Koukl, as well as anyone in modern times, summarizes and elucidates the Bible's grand sweep and shows how it provides the answers to the transcendent philosophical questions that have intrigued and troubled mankind from the beginning. "What is the reason for everything? Why am I here? Why is anything here?"

The author himself doesn't presume to unveil a complete picture of reality as if he personally discovered it in an exclusive epiphany. Rather, he contends that the God-inspired Bible supplies the answers and that they are accessible to all of us because God intended them to be.

The Bible doesn't have to be intimidating. It presents the story of mankind, whose author created human beings in his image to share his infinite love and his happiness with us. It is a unified, integrated account from beginning to end (the end not having yet occurred), and we are all part of the story.

Christianity doesn't begin in Bethlehem with God's entrance into human history 2,000 years ago. Our triune God created humankind and placed us in his wonderfully crafted world knowing in advance that we would corrupt ourselves through sin. "Evil did not catch God by surprise."

Our perfect God knew that to restore mankind to our original state, suitable to being in God's presence throughout eternity, he would have to send his son to become one of us while also retaining his divine nature, suffer the indignities of human existence, live a sinless life, die a sacrificial and substitutionary death for our sins, and be resurrected to life so that by faith in him, we could be redeemed and saved.

Koukl traces the Bible's storyline and demonstrates that "Christianity is a picture of reality. It is an account or a description or a depiction of the way things actually are. It is not just a view from the inside (a Christian's personal feelings or religious beliefs or spiritual affections or ethical views or 'relationship' with God). It is also a view of the outside. It is a view of the world out there, of how the world really is in itself."

But Christianity is not merely one of many possible explanations of reality. It is *the* explanation of how things actually are — of who God is, why he created us, how we blew it (and continue to blow it) when he created us, how he supplied the remedy and how the story ends. In short, the Bible describes the Creation, the Fall, the Redemption and our ultimate restoration.

The Old Testament isn't in the Bible for occasional reference. It contains the beginning of the story, and it relates God's establishment of his chosen nation of Israel through Abraham and God's promise to bless all of mankind through the Messiah, who would come from that nation. The Gospel must be understood in the context of God's entire story for mankind.

Once you understand the story — once you grasp the big picture of reality as laid out in the Bible — you will see that certain thorny problems that were formerly obstacles to your faith need not be obstacles at all. For example, the existence and pervasiveness of evil despite there being an omnipotent and omnibenevolent God are not incomprehensible at all. "Evil is not the problem for Christianity that people think it is," writes Koukl, "because it is not foreign to the Story. It is central to it. It fits right in. In a certain sense, the entire Story is precisely about how the world went bad and how it gets fixed." Paradoxically, evil is a far bigger problem for the atheist than it is for the Christian — but you'll have to read the book to see how Koukl fascinatingly unpacks this.

It is extremely difficult to do justice to such a profound book in a short column, but let me just add that it affirms so much of my own thinking about Scripture and its mind-blowing revelations, which really are within our grasp if we'll just pick up the Bible and read and study it.

The book will facilitate your understanding and accelerate your learning process. It is the most concise, cogent explanation of the Christian message I've encountered since C.S. Lewis' "Mere Christianity." If you are already a believer, it will clarify and reinforce your faith like few books I've read, and if you are not, it might just rock your world.

I have already recommended this amazing work to family and close friends and am now doing the same for all of you. You won't be disappointed.

The Left's All-Out War on Trump

February 17, 2017

Please don't tell us conservatives that we need to find common ground with the left during this era of Trump. That would only advance liberals' cause, because they have no intention of working with President Trump. They are conducting an all-out war against him and his administration, and appeasement efforts wouldn't change that.

What the naive among us need to understand is that the left plays hardball. Liberals subscribe to an end-justifies-the-means philosophy. They are not fair. They don't intend to be fair. They believe they are entitled to advance their America-transforming agenda whether in or out of power, and no amount of wishful thinking can alter that reality.

They will say and do practically anything to further their vision for America, and it doesn't matter if they did the opposite yesterday. A foolish consistency is the hobgoblin of little conservative minds.

The leftist machine purports to be opposed to Trump for his allegedly dastardly actions, but he has barely had time to get started (though he deserves great credit for what he has done so far). Truth be told, liberals' opposition springs not from what he's done — other than the travel ban — but from who he is and the threat he represents to their agenda.

They told us he would be a tyrannical autocrat, and just four weeks into his term, they claim to have him dead to rights on the charge. Yet Trump has not engaged in any illegal conduct or committed any lawless overreaches. President Obama, on the other hand, was habitually lawless, and the left, far from being concerned, reveled in it. Ends and means.

Understand this: The left has no evidence that Trump colluded with Russia to affect our election. It is absurd that we are even forced to talk about this. Smear with innuendo and slander — that's liberals' MO.

In case you haven't noticed, these professional malcontents have organized throughout the nation, with more than a little help from the community organizer in ex-chief, Barack Obama. They have placed themselves throughout the nation to make mischief — not the kind you smile at but the kind designed to bring down a duly elected president.

With remarkable foresight and patience, progressives have conspired for decades to plant themselves in America's important institutions, from the universities to the halls of government in secure civil service jobs. Many of these people are working overtime inside and outside government to undermine, scandalize, sabotage and ultimately bring down the Trump administration in its incipiency. That tactic is a lot easier than trying to block his desperately needed reform agenda on the merits.

I strongly suspect that leftists within our intelligence agencies criminally leaked classified information to corroborate their claim that Trump colluded with Russia to interfere with the presidential election. They thought they'd hit pay dirt with reports that before Trump took office, his national security adviser, Michael Flynn, had conversations with Russian Ambassador Sergey Kislyak allegedly about reviewing the recent sanctions Obama had imposed on Russia.

Can you imagine the salivating? Here's the smoking gun. Flynn talked to Russia. Trump likes Russian President Vladimir Putin. Russia hacked the United States. Trump won the election. Therefore, Trump colluded with Putin to engineer his election victory over Hillary Clinton. That is one convoluted syllogism, isn't it?

The left doesn't care about the truth of the matter. Once liberals obtained what they considered a colorable morsel of damning evidence, they insisted their fears about Trump were already vindicated. He was guilty as charged. Except that he wasn't.

Flynn has stated that his conversation didn't touch on sanctions. The New York Times, in its story reporting that Trump campaign aides had repeated contacts with Russian intelligence agents, admitted it had seen no evidence of cooperation or collusion between the Trump team and the Russians regarding the election. That little tidbit has not found its way into any headline in the mainstream media.

Liberals hate Trump, and they hate that they lost the election, and they are not going to tolerate it. I hope the rest of America understands that.

They are not only disgracefully pretending they have hard evidence of misconduct leading directly to Trump but also ignoring the egregious misconduct of the leakers and the real threat that poses to national security.

Trump got off to an incredibly impressive start, but liberals have now delivered a blow to his momentum, and they are poised to finish the job. They are strategically placed in our cultural institutions and throughout our vast bureaucracy and are coordinating in every state to stage planned protests that look spontaneous. Richly funded by George Soros and other like-minded America haters, they are inspired by the shadow leadership of former President Obama and his activist organization formed for this very purpose.

I will not defend misconduct on the part of elected officials and their appointees — if it actually occurs — just because they are Republicans. But I am not going to sit by silently as the left continues to smear and sabotage this newly inaugurated president based on shards of facts that don't prove their allegations.

I realize that nothing we do will stop the left or dampen its single-minded determination to destroy Trump and preserve Obama's radical agenda, but we can prevent the left from succeeding if we fight back with equal energy and commitment. But that will be impossible unless we fully recognize what's going on — the tactics of the left and liberals' ruthlessness. We are, in effect, in a war that we didn't start.

So please keep your eyes open and prepare to fight back.

In the meantime, let's pray that President Trump will not be unduly distracted by these efforts and can focus on advancing an agenda that will restore economic growth and shore up America's national security. His news conference on Thursday gives me great confidence that President Trump fully understands what the left is doing. He is undeterred and undistracted — and pressing forward with his agenda. The left, in turn, probably now understands that it has unleashed a tiger.

The Pouting and Shouting Left Is Just Being Itself

February 24, 2017

I'd almost forgotten how unreasonable the left can be when out of power, but liberals are giving us a daily refresher course, and it's almost hard to take seriously — except we must.

They describe everything President Donald Trump does in hyperbolic terms. He's a fascist. He's destroying our liberties. He disrespects the rule of law. He represents a threat to humanity. He is going to start a world war. He is a danger to the freedom of the press. He needs to be impeached.

A few quick examples. America did fine for 240 years without a lawless federal mandate requiring all public school districts to allow transgender students to use bathrooms that match their gender identity rather than those that correspond with their actual gender. According to liberals, the world is coming to an end. Trump has dealt a devastating blow to this beleaguered group of people, and he's an ogre. In fact, Trump lawfully reversed a lawless order, which will result in leaving the matter to the states to decide. Far from harming this minuscule group, he is protecting all other people from the concern that they or their children will have to share the same bathroom with those of the opposite gender.

Sunsara Taylor, an activist with Refuse Fascism, appeared on Tucker Carlson's Fox News Channel program to rant maniacally about how Trump and Vice President Mike Pence are operating out of "Hitler's playbook." Trump, she said, "is more dangerous than Hitler ever could have been." She called Trump and Pence a "danger to humanity" but offered no evidence they had done anything to justify her ridiculous charges. From what I could tell, Taylor's main concern is that Trump is trying to advance a conservative agenda while in control of "the biggest nuclear arsenal in the world." Conservatism plus nukes apparently equals a clear and present danger to mankind.

Before you dismiss this as a one-off exception to normally rational behavior, consider that Rep. Keith Ellison of Minnesota — who is vying to be chairman of the Democratic National Committee, no less — said he is open to calls to begin impeachment proceedings against Trump. "I think that Donald Trump has already done a number of things which legitimately raise the question of impeachment," said Ellison. And Ellison is not an outlier. Rep. Maxine Waters, D-Calif., also called for Trump's impeachment, describing Trump's team as "a bunch of scumbags."

Such lovely tolerant liberals took to social media to attack first lady Melania Trump, mocking her accent and religion — some calling her a whore, others a hostage — because she recited the Lord's Prayer at a campaign rally.

The glaring irony with all this is that it is liberals who are hateful and intolerant, authoritarian and lawless. They are the ones who represent a threat to our liberties — not Trump, Republicans or conservatives.

It's worth noting that almost every charge these breathless critics make against Trump is baseless and grounded on their irrational fears of what he might do rather than anything he's done. It's also remarkable that though these concerns are exaggerated when applied to Trump, many of them could have been accurately applied to President Barack Obama.

The dirty big non-secret is that the left isn't concerned about the rule of law or any alleged threats to liberty. Liberals are pouting (and shouting) because for once in their lifetimes, they are not getting their way. For once, someone in a position of authority is refusing to roll over to political correctness. For once, a powerful public official is holding his hands up against this bullying liberal juggernaut and saying: "Stop. We've had enough. The people have had enough. You are not going to steamroll us anymore. We aren't any longer going to look the other way when you ignore the law, when you use the courts and unaccountable administrative agencies to legislate your will, when you use holdover federal bureaucrats to thwart the will of the chief executive and when your biased media distort the facts and advocate a liberal agenda rather than objectively report the news. We are not going to cower at the demagogic cabal that says people aren't paying their fair share of taxes. We aren't going to be shamed as heartless or nativists for demanding secure borders and safe cities. We aren't going to accept your belittling for identifying the enemy, by name, that is at war with us and with Western civilization. We aren't going to accede to your narrative that radical Islamic terrorists are only at war with us because we provoke them, so we reject your mindless mantra that the prison at Guantanamo Bay is a recruiting tool for otherwise peaceful global citizens. We aren't going to passively ignore your own selective assaults on religious liberty — on Christians. We aren't going to continue to allow you to dominate the public dialogue. We're finally fighting back — not as some tit-for-tat pettiness but because we believe that we are doing the right thing, that your virtual monopoly on the culture has been devastating and that it's time to begin reversing the destruction you've wrought.

"But unlike you, we won't break the law in undoing your agenda and advancing ours. To us, the ends don't justify the means. We won't — despite your projected concerns — diminish the freedom of the press or the constitutional liberties of any other individuals or groups. We are going to aggressively pursue policies that are in the best interests of America and the American people. Please keep calling us crazy and displaying your true colors to the American people, and with any luck, we'll do even better in 2020, provided we persevere in standing up to your bullying and proceed with a pro-growth, pro-defense, pro-liberty agenda."

Trump's Speech Was an A-plus

March 3, 2017

I was unable to watch President Trump's speech to Congress in real time but heard it was phenomenal. I watched it the next day, and it was even better than I expected.

There was enough meat in the first five minutes to satisfy a hungry audience of Americans and fuel an extensive column, but it just kept getting better.

I don't agree that Trump became presidential for the first time that evening as so many opined in chorus, because I think he's been presidential since his inauguration and also because I don't subscribe to the commentariat's superficial concept of presidentiality; to me, it's not a matter of creased pants but an attitude and reverence for the office.

The speech was powerful and precisely what the American people needed to hear, given the incessant liberal media barrage against the administration and person of Donald Trump since he was elected.

The contrast between this speech and the typical Obama speech couldn't be greater. Obama's addresses invariably involved these themes: scapegoating his predecessor and Republican opposition, offering empty platitudes of hope and change with few specifics, acute avoidance of personal accountability, willful blindness and denial concerning the identity of our terrorist enemy, deliberately destructive divisiveness, subtle shaming of America for alleged past and present sins, disrespect for America's founding ideals, wholesale obliviousness to the notion of the uniqueness of America's liberty tradition and the very notion of liberty, a dangerously distorted view of America's perpetual economic malaise and joblessness on his watch, a maddening indifference to our national debt, quasi idolatry toward a mythical and fraudulent consensus about so-called man-made climate change, an overt betrayal of America's energy industry, a slavish addiction to taxes and regulations as a panacea for our ills, the cruel lie that high-quality, affordable universal health care is achievable, and the disturbing drumbeat of war against America's corporations, small businesses and entrepreneurs.

President Trump's speech, on the other hand, was truly uplifting — but not because of eloquent promises of vague future blessings or because it was well-delivered. In fact, I think observers are placing undue emphasis on Trump's presidential delivery and demeanor, though he deserves high marks on those. Americans are finally past the point of being seduced by eloquent turns of phrase. They're looking for real solutions — ideas that work in the real world and not just in the fantasy world of arrogant academic theoreticians. Content and substance are key, not smoke and mirrors — and Trump delivered.

He set the tone with a series of assurances that he is not the bigoted ogre depicted by the mainstream media. Right off the bat, he addressed minorities and the cause of civil rights and laid down a marker signaling that the Republican Party intends to proactively address problems particularly affecting minority communities in the inner cities. He pointedly decried the recent incidents of vandalism against Jewish centers and denounced "hate and evil, in all of its very ugly forms," and then he segued into expressing a firm commitment — "deeply delivered from (his) heart" — to unify and improve the lives of all Americans through a vigorous renewal of the American spirit.

He dispelled concerns about his allegiance to our allies, underscoring that he honors our mutual relationships but is determined to reinstitute America's proper leadership role.

Possibly most uplifting to me were his promise to keep America strong and free — concepts you rarely heard from President Obama — and his exaltation of America's founding principles, all without recriminations toward any group about the lack of fairness or social justice.

To the chagrin of the leftist-dominated Democratic Party, Trump voiced genuine concern for the neglect of our inner cities and the decline of the middle class. He gave us straight talk about the myths Democrats have fed Americans for the past eight years about the economy and jobs, reminding us that millions upon millions of Americans are out of the workforce, food stamps are at a record high and we've had the worst economic recovery in 65 years. Americans deserve the truth, and they deserve better.

Unlike his predecessor, Trump did not engage in demagoguery. He didn't demonize certain groups while promising selective relief for others. He promoted equal opportunity and equal justice for all, irrespective of ethnicity, creed, color or gender.

Refreshingly, he reiterated his commitment to veterans and his unwavering pledge to rebuild our military and our neglected inner cities. Unapologetically, he doubled down on his policy to thoroughly vet people entering this country, properly noting that it was not compassionate but reckless to allow potential killers into our nation. Proudly, he announced his support of the coal and oil industries and his goal of American energy independence.

He promised substantial corporate and middle-class tax cuts to spur economic growth and provide relief for Americans and American businesses. He reassured us that he is adamant about disentangling America from the regulatory chokehold it has been under for decades, and he offered specifics to effectuate that promise.

He restated his priority to restore the rule of law to our courts and our cities, which have too often descended into chaos.

Finally, I couldn't help but notice Trump's obviously intended emphasis on reviewing his many campaign promises, detailing his fulfillment of some and dedication to honor the remainder. This may have represented his most marked departure from the Obama era. It was a veritable invitation for us to shine the light of personal accountability on him — something we never saw from President Obama and wouldn't have seen even if he could have served another five full terms.

President Trump has given us notice that he intends to do what he said he would do and to subject himself to scrutiny on those promises — while calling out those whose singular goal is to obstruct him.

I am not saying the speech was perfect or that I agree with every Trump policy, but I am saying it was a delightfully invigorating, inspiring and reassuring speech — and one that sustains my hope that it is indeed morning in America again.

Free Market Solutions the
Key to Health Care Reform

March 10, 2017

Health care reform is an enormous challenge because when it comes to economic policy, Republicans always have an uphill battle. Their free market solutions are harder to sell in a nation that has long had one foot in the socialism door.

Republicans express their belief in the free market, especially when they're out of power and running against liberals and their failed policies, but they have a tougher time governing on conservative principles once in office. They often operate on flawed assumptions, seeking to accomplish contradictory goals and operating in an environment with two-year election cycles, which discourage making correct decisions for the long term.

But the GOP must recapture its belief in free market principles and muster the patience and political courage to promote them. Competition and free markets are the best avenues to economic prosperity, liberty and, in the case of health care, accessibility, affordability and quality. Yes, we must support some kind of safety net, but it ought to be designed to be short-term in as many cases as possible and should create incentives to encourage people to help themselves.

Some critics rightly note that Obamacare and other forms of socialized medicine are elaborate redistribution schemes, and that is true, as far as it goes. But our economy is dynamic; it is not a zero-sum game. Liberals conveniently ignore that their redistribution schemes, when extended to their logical conclusion, don't just reallocate resources. Overregulation smothers market forces and destroys wealth, liberty and human dignity, and it is ruining American health care. It's a shame that such issues rarely find their way into the public debate because it's easier just to appear compassionate.

Indeed, it's easy to be an economic liberal who pretends to care only about the poor. But feelings don't translate into results and often sabotage them. The welfare system has diminished the work ethic, increased the incentive for people to reproduce out of wedlock and severely damaged the nuclear family, which has led to incalculable economic, moral and cultural problems across the board.

Republicans need to be more serious than the compassion-peddling Democrats and decide what they are trying to accomplish with health care reform. Why do people accept Barack Obama's premise that health insurance coverage, rather than quality affordable health care, is the end goal? More Americans are technically covered today, but premiums and deductibles have increased, and quality has decreased.

Democrats, starting with the Clintons in the 1990s, changed the conversation to insurance coverage with the mantra that we had tens of millions uninsured. Lost in the conversation was any concern for premiums, deductibles, accessibility of care and quality of care. Though Hillary Clinton didn't have the cachet to get Hillarycare passed, Obama crammed his warped vision down our throats.

But like all other socialistic solutions, Obamacare was terminally flawed. Government intervention was already the biggest enemy of quality affordable health care, and Obamacare was just another cynical weigh station on the way to single-payer, fully socialized medicine.

Health care is a complex issue, and its complexity increases along with greater government intervention, which makes reforming it quite difficult. We must begin by rejecting the assumptions that health insurance is a constitutional right and that medical services can be free. We don't need health insurance for every routine medical procedure, as opposed to bigger or catastrophic items, because insurance is about unforeseen risks and routine procedures are foreseen. And when we insist on coverage for those with pre-existing conditions, can we at least be honest that we are also violating the concept of insurance?

Though I don't pretend to be an expert on the specifics, I am convinced that principles of free market competition must infuse any health care reforms we ultimately adopt. This means eliminating as many regulations as we can, removing barriers to competition across state lines, implementing tort reform, allowing unlimited health savings accounts and somehow disentangling ourselves from a system in which the health care consumer pays only 11 percent of his own health care costs, with the remainder being paid by employers and other third parties. Under the present system, people have no incentive to be prudent and frugal consumers, and providers have no incentive to reduce costs.

In fairness, we must also concede that accomplishing such reforms legislatively is extremely difficult. It's infinitely easier to advocate full repeal or "repeal and replace" when you're the opposition party. But achieving reform in a democratic system designed to retard legislative action is a different animal. We don't even have a consensus on the Republican side, and the Democrats are and will remain in full obstruction mode.

Critics must soberly acknowledge the immense difficulty of such reforms and have some appreciation for pragmatic considerations, such as passing what we can through the reconciliation process, which only requires a simple majority, and advancing other items separately, if necessary. We can't just snap our fingers and get things done.

I am somewhat conflicted on this because part of me believes we should just repeal the whole thing and be done with it, but the other part is aware of the difficulty of getting a consensus to actually pass legislation.

I think House Speaker Paul Ryan and others deserve credit for trying to move this in the right direction, but I am still concerned that the American Health Care Act wouldn't go far enough or fast enough — especially when economists and conservative think tanks I trust are very skeptical of the plan. We must understand that piecemeal solutions regularly create greater problems down the road, which we've seen with the problems created by the expansion of Medicaid in some 31 states. Once you increase people's and states' dependence on the federal government, it is harder to wean them off on the road to true market reforms.

My hope is that we approach this and any other proposed reform legislation skeptically, but not cynically, and that we evaluate it in terms of whether it would advance health care in the short term and long term — toward a market-based system, which is the surest and best way to achieve affordable high-quality health care. If the American Health Care Act, along with the next two phases of legislation, can eventually accomplish that, I'll be for it, but the jury is still out.

Judge Watson's Abominable
Travel Ban Ruling

March 17, 2017

Anyone who understands the modern left could not be shocked by U.S. District Judge Derrick Watson's issuance of a temporary restraining order against President Donald Trump's executively invoked travel ban — but that doesn't make the order any less outrageous.

The ruling was not just an exercise in judicial tyranny, as many have commented, but an act of jurisprudential nihilism and anarchy. Courts are not policymaking bodies but judicial tribunals that decide actual disputes on the basis of the facts and the law.

For decades, the courts have arrogated to themselves the power to act outside their constitutional authority by usurping the legislative function of writing and rewriting, rather than interpreting, laws and adjudicating their constitutionality.

Judicial activism overwhelmingly comes from left-wing judges, many of whom see their role as advancing a progressive policy agenda and exhibit little respect for the Constitution and rule of law when they might interfere with that agenda.

When President Trump issued his original travel ban, it was wholly predictable that some court would attempt to nullify it. In that case, its job was made easier by the arguable clumsiness of the rollout, even though most honest commentators believed that the underlying order passed constitutional muster.

Phony critics pretended the ban was stricken only because it was illegally crafted and opined that had Trump used greater care in composing the order, he would have faced no judicial obstacles.

Others recognized this as a convenient excuse and said Trump would not be able to circumvent judicial obstruction merely by drafting a more precise order.

Alas, when the president issued a new order, it suffered the same fate as the first. Once a plaintiff was recruited for the cause, it wasn't hard to find a court to eradicate Trump Travel Ban 2.0.

What was less predictable, though, was the transparent speciousness of the court's reasoning in striking down Trump's lawful order. A self-respecting judge would be embarrassed by this sophistry, unless he derived his professional self-concept from his devotion to political causes through bastardization of his sworn judicial oath.

Chief Justice John Marshall, in establishing the judiciary's prerogative of judicial review in the 1803 case Marbury v. Madison, said, "It is emphatically the province and duty of the judicial department to say what the law is." He did not say, "The judiciary is superior to the legislative and executive branches, and accordingly, we have the right to just make stuff up."

Yet that's precisely what Judge Watson did. He issued the temporary restraining order mainly because the executive order purportedly violated the establishment clause, which Watson reduced to this formulation: "The clearest command of the Establishment Clause is that one religious denomination cannot be officially preferred over another." But even Watson admitted it is undisputed that the order "does not facially discriminate for or against any particular religion, or for or against religion versus non-religion." So it's not Trump's executive order that arguably violates the establishment clause; it's his alleged intent behind the order, which Trump supposedly revealed in his statements during the presidential campaign and otherwise concerning Muslims.

The judge says that to determine whether the order violates this clause, a court must apply the three-part "Lemon test." To show it has not run afoul of the clause, the government action must satisfy all three prongs of the test: 1) It must have a primary secular purpose. 2) It may not have the principal effect of advancing or inhibiting religion. 3) It may not foster excessive entanglement with religion.

Watson concluded that the order fails the first test — the "secular purpose" prong — so a court wouldn't even have to consider the other two tests. But it is painfully obvious that the primary purpose of Trump's executive order is secular; he has exercised his sovereign duty to protect Americans and America's national security interests. It is laughable and outrageous to suggest there was any other purpose — much less a religiously discriminatory purpose — to invoke the order.

On Page 32 of his 43-page screed, Watson cited the 9th U.S. Circuit Court of Appeals' ruling that "official action that targets religious conduct for distinctive treatment cannot be shielded by mere compliance with the requirement of facial neutrality."

But nothing in the order targets religious conduct for distinctive treatment! The order doesn't address any aspect of Muslim religious conduct, unless Watson was arguing that terrorism is protected religious conduct. The ban applies to just six nations whose entrants are believed to present a higher risk of harm to the United States. This is not about religion but about national security. The five pillars of Islam are wholly unthreatened by Trump's order.

Particularly disingenuous was Watson's statement, on Page 36, that "any reasonable, objective observer would conclude ... that the stated secular purpose of the Executive Order is, at the very least, 'secondary to a religious objective' of temporarily suspending the entry of Muslims." This is astonishing, even for a radical jurist. No reasonable person — apart from a mixed-up, virtue-signaling leftist — would conclude that the stated secular purpose is secondary. If you're going to consider Trump's statements, he is nothing if not a national security hawk. Moreover, Americans who voted for him based on national security concerns see this order as a national security imperative. They know, even if pointy-headed leftist judges do not, that presidents have a duty to protect the United States and that the greatest threat to its national security presently is from terrorists. I repeat: There is no religious objective to this order at all, much less a primary one. It doesn't apply just to Muslims, and it doesn't "target religious conduct" of Muslims.

On top of all this, Watson conceded that to issue the temporary restraining order, he had to determine that the plaintiffs had met their burden of establishing a strong likelihood of success on the merits of their claim, yet he never explained how there is a small likelihood, much less a strong likelihood, of success, especially considering that this would be, according to liberal Harvard law professor Alan Dershowitz, a case of first impression.

The judge has written 43 pages of words — just words — designed to obfuscate the issue and justify the unjustifiable judicial usurpation of the sovereign power of the executive branch over national security.

This will not stand. Watson's order cannot stand.

Princeton Seminary Disses
Pastor Timothy Keller

Match 24, 2017

Can we all agree that modern leftists tend to politicize everything they can get their hands on — in every venue? Even the sacred isn't sacred.

Princeton Theological Seminary reversed its decision to bestow the annual Abraham Kuyper Prize to New York City pastor Timothy Keller — for essentially political reasons.

Keller leads an enormously popular Reformed church in the heart of New York City. Before you challenge popularity as a meaningful yardstick for evaluating a pastor, know that his popularity is not based on straying from Scripture or Christian principles, but on being faithful to them.

Yes, even in New York City there is obviously a deep spiritual hunger for the truth and that is what Keller and his church provide, in spades.

I am familiar with Keller and his preaching, as I own several of his books and his entire sermon archive, which I purchased through Logos Bible Software — an amazing resource that I've used to research my Christian-themed books. I have visited Keller's church, and though he wasn't preaching that day, the pastor who was delivered a biblical, Christ-centered message without a hint of politics.

Neither in Keller's writings nor his sermons have I detected the slightest inclination toward the political. He preaches the Gospel and the entire Bible with clarity and inspiration. His insights are invaluable and routinely profound. He is truly gifted and seems to practice the Christlike humility he preaches, not seeking to make himself a celebrity or otherwise leverage his talents to redirect the focus from Scripture to himself.

His disqualifying sin was not that he joined the now defunct Moral Majority or publicly endorsed some evil Republican politician. Nor was it that he rejected any of the church's doctrinal tenets. It was not that his teachings might lead people away from the church's mission to spread the Gospel. Rather, it was apparently his refusal to deviate from Scripture and conform his teachings to the current liberal political line on certain hot-button issues.

Certain people raised Cain about Keller's "conservative positions" and the seminary decided it better renege on offering the award. Keller is a leader in the Presbyterian Church in America, which, according to Princeton Theological Seminary President Craig Barnes, "prevents women and LGBTQ+ persons from full participation in the ordained Ministry of Word and Sacrament." The Seminary is part of a different denomination — the Presbyterian Church (USA), whose position on this issue conflicts with Keller and the PCA.

"Many regard awarding the Kuyper Prize as affirmation of Reverend Keller's belief that women and LGBTQ+ persons should not be ordained. This conflicts with the stance of the Presbyterian Church (USA). And it is an important issue among the divided Reformed communions."

The Kuyper Prize is "awarded each year to a scholar or community leader whose outstanding contribution to their chosen sphere reflects the ideas and values characteristic of the Neo-Calvinist vision of religious engagement in matters of social, political and cultural significance in one or more of the spheres of society."

Keller apparently satisfied the criteria when he was chosen, but the ubiquitous forces of political correctness and social justice would have none of it. So Keller got the axe.

Keller won't get the award, but not to worry — he'll still get the consolation prize of being allowed to speak at the school's annual conference in April.

Ah, liberal tolerance — it's everywhere.

Keller is especially worthy of such an honor and the school's action is disgraceful. "If you can't give an Abraham Kuyper award to Tim Keller," asked Southern Baptist leader Daniel Darling, "who can you give it to?"

Even in the church and church-affiliated institutions, those who subscribe to biblical views on marriage, even universally respected Christian leaders, must be scorned. The Bible and those entrusted with teaching it must yield to the moral strictures of the culture.

People sometimes ask what Christians and conservatives can do to reverse the relentless advance of secularism, progressivism and moral relativism in our culture. Well, they can start by waking up to the reality of the ongoing attacks on biblical and traditional values and the vilification of those who openly embrace them. They can quit ignoring these assaults because they prefer to avoid controversy. The truth is often controversial and should not take a back seat to pseudo concerns for harmony articulated by those who daily sew seeds of discord unless you unquestionably submit to their views.

The Bible should be our guide, not the shifting currents of political correctness and the bullying demands of leftist malcontents. Pastor Timothy Keller will not be harmed by this rejection. This good and faithful servant has already received an infinitely higher award.

Four Days in Israel Verify
Biblical Places and Events

March 31, 2017

I have wanted to visit the Holy Land for years and I am finally here. The experience is, as promised, exceeding my enormously high expectations. Finally, I can use the word "awesome" correctly and without exaggeration!

This is a 10-day tour organized by Living Passages and led by my friend, Christian apologetics author and speaker Frank Turek, of CrossExamined.org. We are visiting mostly Old Testament-related sites on the first part of the trip and those of the New Testament on the second part.

There are 35 of us in the group, and we are traveling from site to site on a bus with Israeli tour guide Eli Shukron, an accomplished archaeologist whose prominent Jerusalem discoveries include the pool of Siloam and tunnels under the City of David. Eli has a passion for making the Bible come alive by explaining the geography, history, and biblical significance of the sites we are touring. Turek is complementing these teachings with his unique biblical and apologetic messages.

One thing that greatly distinguishes the Bible from other ancient religious texts is that the historical events and geographical locations it describes can often be verified. Let me just share a bit about the major locations we've visited in the first few days of our journey.

As we flew into Tel Aviv at midday, I was taken by the beauty of the land. We spent our first night in Ashdod, Israel's largest port, located on the Mediterranean coast. Ashdod is where the Philistines took the ark of the covenant after they defeated the Israelites. The first book of Samuel relates that they placed the ark in the temple of their god Dagon and set it beside Dagon's statue. The next morning, the statue fell face downward before the ark, evidencing God's judgment on the Philistines for stealing the ark.

The Lord also afflicted the people of Ashdod with tumors, convincing them to return the ark to the Israelites after having it only seven months. They returned it by cart to the Israelite city of Beth-Shemesh, east of Ashdod. Our group traveled from Ashdod to Beth-Shemesh, where we visited the excavation of Khirbet Qeiyafa nearby. Here we walked through the impressive ruins of a well-planned, fortified urban city established during the time of King David (circa 1000 B.C.), which has been validated by carbon dating and pottery of that period.

Archaeologists also discovered miniature structures that looked like Solomon's Temple and might have been models for the future temple. This city is believed to be the biblical city of Shaaraim (1 Sam. 17:52), which means "two gates." Our guide, Eli, was animated in showing us both the eastern and western gates, which were clearly detectable even today. Large parts of the stone foundations of many houses within the city walls were still in place. From the high vantage point of the city we looked down on the valley of Elah, where David killed Goliath (1 Sam. 17). It is moving to stand in the very spot where these historical events occurred and it gives a richer significance to the biblical accounts.

We next visited the active archaeological site Tel Mareshah, where we were invited to participate in the dig. One member of our group discovered an oil lamp dated around 300 B.C.

From there we went to the site of the ancient city of Lachish, which was originally conquered by Joshua and later was second only to Jerusalem in strategic importance to Judah, whose king, Rehoboam, fortified the city for the defense of his kingdom (2 Chronicles 11:9).

The Assyrians had already conquered the Northern Kingdom of Israel in 722 B.C. and had their sights set on the southern kingdom of Judah. Accordingly, Assyrian King Sennacherib invaded Judah and conquered Lachish in 701 B.C. He memorialized this victory with a series of reliefs that he had carved on his palace walls in Nineveh, which depicted the siege and capture of Lachish (2 Kings

18:14, 17; 19:8; 2 Chronicles 32:9; Isaiah 36:2; 37; 37:8; Micah 1:13). Those reliefs are now in the British Museum.

When Sennacherib put siege to Jerusalem, as the Bible says, he couldn't overtake the city. While not claiming victory, Sennacherib bragged that he had Judah's King "Hezekiah caged like a bird" on the ancient Taylor Prism found in Iraq in 1830. This Prism is also in the British Museum and is verification of another event in the Bible.

It is difficult to express the majesty of these ancient areas and to adequately explain their profound impact. Though I have read and studied the Old Testament, I can't begin to describe how much more meaningful its stories are after walking the grounds on which they unfolded. We have barely begun our journey and it is already the trip of my lifetime. Nothing else compares. In a later column, I'll tell you about the New Testament sites we visit.

The True Jesus

April 14, 2017

I have a new book out — "The True Jesus," which is my third Christian-themed book — and I want to tell you a little bit about it.

In my previous books, I related that I didn't always embrace the Bible and that I came to accept Jesus Christ later than some people do — after studying the evidence for Christianity's truth claims. Contrary to a common misconception, there is an abundance of evidence that undergirds the Christian faith, and I examined much of that in my previous books.

This book is different in that it allows the Gospels to speak for themselves, as they are their own best apologetic.

I have developed a deep passion for the Bible and theology over the years, and I want to share that to help teach people about it and inspire them to read it. I initially intended this to be a sort of layman's guide to the New Testament, having focused on the Old Testament in my most recent book. But as I began writing, it became clear to me that I couldn't cover the entire New Testament in as much depth as I wanted, so I decided to narrow the scope to the Gospels alone.

When you read the Gospels with an open mind and heart, you will discover that you are encountering Jesus — walking with him, observing him in action, and sitting at his feet and listening to his teachings. It is impossible to read these four books without recognizing that they are describing a being so sublime that no human author or group of authors could have conceived him. The Gospel writers — Matthew, Mark, Luke and John — repeatedly report that the crowds were amazed at his teachings. The officers who returned on a failed assignment to arrest Jesus explained, "No one ever spoke like this man!"

Jesus exuded deity and sinless perfection from every fiber of his being, but he was also fully human. Understanding both aspects of his nature is critical to understanding who he is and what he did for us. But you won't fully grasp this unless you read the Bible for yourself.

Sadly, some people are intimidated by the Bible or don't know where to begin. That is where books about the Bible can be helpful. They are no substitute for the real thing, but they sometimes help ready people for the Word.

My book is a primer on the Gospels designed to inspire reluctant readers to read these four books for themselves and to help others learn more about them and dig deeper into them.

It includes two sections, the first — chapters 1 through 4 — being an introduction to the Gospels. In addition to looking at the basics of the Gospels in this section, I explore the history of the Promised Land during the 400 years between the end of the Old Testament period and Christ's birth. The Jewish people had been released from captivity and returned to their land and were trying to restore their relationship with God while a succession of foreign empires dominated them and controlled the land. I also examine the providential confluence of events that made this the perfect time for Jesus to enter into human history and for the spread of the Gospel message. The Roman Empire brought relative peace to the land, and its roads facilitated travel. The Greek language and culture permeated all the lands of the empire.

In the second and main section of the book — chapters 5 through 12 — I combine the Gospels into a unified, roughly chronological account. I don't try to harmonize the four books, which I consider a fool's errand, because it is not really feasible to do that. But I do believe it is helpful to consolidate them in a work such as this for the limited purpose of exposing readers to all the events recorded in the Gospels.

So I have tried to include every event that occurred and every teaching Jesus imparted, providing commentary along with each event, trying to give readers more insight into Jesus' words and deeds.

I have sometimes paraphrased for space purposes, always careful to stay true to the text, but I have included most of Jesus' words verbatim. Please believe me that my purpose was not to tinker with God's Word, which cannot be improved upon, but to expose readers to the entirety of the Gospels, help accelerate their learning curve and, most of all, inspire them to delve into the Gospels themselves.

My prayer is that by reading this book, you will acquire or reacquire a passion for the Gospels and for Jesus Christ, learn more about him, and resolve to study the Gospels on your own. Though they can mostly be understood even by children, there is no end to their depth of riches and their ability to transform our lives.

The Case for Christ

April 21, 2017

As most of you doubtlessly know, Lee Strobel has a new movie out, "The Case for Christ," which is based on his blockbuster book with the same title. This movie is fabulous.

I began my search for Christ as a believer in God but not necessarily in the God of the Bible. But my friend Lee was even further from God. He was an outright atheist. This movie shows how Lee was on a mission to disprove Christianity's truth claims and bring his recently converted wife to her senses and ended up being slayed by the evidence.

Lee was an awarding-winning legal journalist at the Chicago Tribune and thought Christianity to be a myth, and he thought his wife, Leslie, was cheating on him by chasing after Christ. He was married to her, not some fictional being created by weak, needy people.

Frustrated, Lee shared his problem with certain colleagues and asked for their advice. He was beside himself as his wife sank deeper and deeper into this Christian vortex. His friends told him to be patient — that things would work out.

Lee decided to put his investigative skills to work and began his research, which included interviewing some of the most respected theologians to investigate their claims. But he also researched liberal scholarship and that of atheists and agnostics. He thought he could knock out this little task inside of a weekend but got more than he'd bargained for. He was shocked to discover that the conservative Christian scholars were thoughtful, intelligent people who were well aware of the skeptics' arguments against Christianity. He threw everything at them, challenging them, often provocatively — but respectfully.

Some two years — not two days — later, he found himself losing the battle because he had discovered that it would require more faith to maintain his atheism than to believe that Jesus was the Son of God. He had difficulty conceding defeat, but he finally decided that a good jury must render a verdict, and he surrendered to his intellectual honesty — and then to Jesus Christ.

His research led him to historical evidence and consideration of cosmology, physics, biochemistry, genetics and human consciousness.

What about the New Testament manuscripts? Surely, our existing copies, what few remain, are unreliable. To the contrary, he discovered that the manuscript evidence for Christianity is abundant. There are more copies of the New Testament than any other ancient document, including the classics whose authenticity we don't give a second thought. We have but a handful of copies of most ancient documents, compared with almost 6,000 copies of the New Testament. A notable exception is Homer's "Iliad," but the number of copies pales in comparison with those we possess of the New Testament.

Surely, there was a major time gap between the existing New Testament copies and the original writings. Here again, Lee's hopes were dashed.

What about the New Testament writers? Weren't they just self-serving zealots whose kooky view about Jesus happened to prevail over competing versions of the story? No. What is fiction is this idea that there were seriously competing versions of the story of Jesus during the first century that were vying for prominence. Moreover, the essential propositions of the Gospels were circulating in verbal form just years after Jesus' death. It wasn't until the second century that Gnosticism seriously reared its head, and even when it did, it was no competition for the Gospels.

Try as he might, Lee could not find a chink in Christianity's armor. He was drowning in the sea of evidence but still resisted. He kept hoping that he would achieve some breakthrough and get his beloved wife back. But it was not to happen.

He didn't have an earth-shattering epiphany. Rather, it was the cumulative weight of the evidence that tipped the scales for him. But the linchpin was the Resurrection. This makes sense, because it wasn't until the disciples encountered Jesus in his bodily form after his death that they finally gave their lives to him. At that point, they were transformed from cowardly skeptics to bold advocates for Christ who gave their lives to spread his good news.

It also makes sense because even the Apostle Paul tells us that if the Resurrection didn't occur, then Christians are to be pitied the most among people. They would die in their sins for a falsehood. But then, the Resurrection did occur, and because of it, we, too, can be resurrected to eternal life with Jesus Christ.

Through Lee's agonizing two-year quest, Leslie remained patient, loving and, most of all, busy in prayer, asking that Lee's resistance would give way to his rational faculties and to the Holy Spirit.

The moment he tells his wife is probably the climax of the movie — extremely touching, moving and real. And it was eminently gratifying to watch this on-screen.

I can't say enough good things about this highly realistic movie. It's not corny or preachy as, sadly, some Christian movies are. The actors portraying Lee and Leslie are real and convincing.

I would encourage every one of you — believers and nonbelievers — to go see this movie. You will witness the power of God touching the heart of a genuinely wonderful human being — Lee Strobel, who has since used his gifts to spread the Word like few other people I know. Bless Lee and Leslie Strobel for this tremendous film and for their work to spread the message of salvation through faith in Jesus Christ.

Liberal Thought Police Getting Scarier

April 28, 2017

The totalitarian left is emboldened by its selective suppression of speech. Just as scary is the deluded thought process that inspires its Stalinism.

Recognizing its inability to compete in the marketplace of ideas, the left has been chipping away for years at the concept of free speech. You have to give leftists points for cleverness, not to mention persistence, because they don't openly advocate censoring conservative speech as such. They pretend to be protecting some greater good or preventing imminent harm to certain groups.

When they failed in talk radio, they resurrected the Fairness Doctrine, which is euphemistically disguised as a policy to ensure the presentation of all viewpoints but is actually a sinister ploy to dilute the power of conservative talk. They always have some excuse — and plausible deniability.

They protest conservative speakers or those easily demonized as conservatives on college campuses, arguing that conservative "hate speech" can lead to violence against certain groups. No one wants violence, so we must muzzle conservative political speech, right?

But it's patently absurd to contend that everyday conservative speech is "hate speech" and that it leads to violence. It is pernicious nonsense. What's worse is that these speech cops don't acknowledge their own hypocrisy in committing violence — the very harm they claim to be preventing — to prevent speech that allegedly could lead to violence. Let's just burn some buildings down and smash some skulls in to show just how adamant we are about preventing violence. I wish I were exaggerating.

But the thought control zealots are now coming up with even more bizarre rationalizations to curb competitive speech. In a recent New York Times op-ed, New York University provost Ulrich Baer argues: "The idea of freedom of speech does not mean a blanket permission to say anything anybody thinks. It means balancing the inherent value of a given view with the obligation to ensure that other members of a given community can participate in discourse as fully recognized members of that community. Free-speech protections — not only but especially in universities, which aim to educate students in how to belong to various communities — should not mean that someone's humanity, or their right to participate in political speech as political agents, can be freely attacked, demeaned or questioned."

You may consider that to be psychobabble. What would you expect from an academic who describes himself in the same piece as "a scholar of literature, history and politics"? But I digress.

Let's try to decipher what he's saying. To do so, we must understand that like so many leftists, Baer cannot avoid viewing these matters through the grid of identity politics; everything must be evaluated in terms of how it affects minorities or historically oppressed groups.

Even though one could define unfettered freedom of expression as "guaranteeing the robust debate from which the truth emerges," we shouldn't support it, Baer also says in the piece. Specifically, we shouldn't protect speech that insults whole groups in an effort to discredit and delegitimize them "as less worthy of participation in the public exchange of ideas." He seems to be saying that if you discredit groups of people with your speech, then you unlevel the playing field to the point that any speech these groups express will be less valuable and effective.

We must weigh the "inherent value" of ideas against the dangerous possibility that these ideas could discredit other groups and thereby effectively silence them, he says. Thus, a "pure model of free speech" presents a "clear and present" danger to our democracy.

So the republic is better-served if we allow certain ivory tower elites, with their worldly wisdom, to weigh the "inherent value" of speech to determine whether it should be protected. If it arguably demeans a certain group — and there are newly defined groups all the time in the left's world — it is not worthy of protection.

Thus, the liberal thought police can decree that because anything conservative firebrand Ann Coulter would say at Berkeley on immigration or other topics would diminish other groups, it should not be protected. She's a conservative, and conservative ideas don't have much inherent value to liberals and, in their distorted world, also discredit certain groups. Voila! Shut her down. The sophistry is astounding.

I urge you not to miss the most stunning aspect of Baer's specious analysis. The thrust of the left's message against conservatives across the board is that because of our toxic ideas, we should be discredited and delegitimized "as less worthy of participation in the public exchange of ideas."

Just as leftists support the commission of violence in the name of preventing speech that could arguably lead to it, they would muzzle us because through our speech, we would discredit and then effectively muzzle them. Insanity.

We don't want to muzzle liberals; we want to defeat them in the marketplace of ideas. We don't want to commit violence against them, but they often want to do so against us. Boy, how they project.

Let me ask you: In their world, who would decide whether certain speech has inherent value? The federal government, no doubt, provided Democrats are in control at the time. The true acid test of Baer's preposterous arguments would be to ask how liberals would feel if Republicans were allowed to make such decisions while in control of the federal government. How would they feel if a conservative had written this silly, scary op-ed?

It is precisely because we can't have certain self-appointed groups deciding what speech is worthy that we must vigorously protect "robust" political speech in this country. The Founding Fathers knew this, and everyone with common sense understands it. But the crazy modern left wants us to unlearn it — and leftists call us conservatives a danger to democracy.

Whatever you do, don't casually dismiss Baer's ideas as fringe. This is the way leftists think today — and they are the people teaching our university students, producing Hollywood movies and largely controlling the mainstream media. Wake up and be vigilant! And fight back!

Thank You, Stephen Colbert

May 5, 2017

I oppose the push to remove "The Late Show" comedian Stephen Colbert from the air because of his obscene tirade against President Donald Trump. In fact, I wish the video of his boorish diatribe would go viral.

The best remedy against the political left's ongoing crusade to remake America in its own vulgar image is maximum exposure of its irrationality. If you haven't seen Colbert's rant, please watch it. It's titled "This Monologue Goes Out To You, Mr. President" on YouTube. There was nothing funny about it; there was nothing clever. It was just one shallow insult after another.

I fail to understand the appeal of these obnoxious, mean-spirited leftist comics whose fawning, sheeplike audiences are about as discriminating as a glutton at a buffet table. They wouldn't clap more if responding to applause cards — but, in fairness, that's probably because they wouldn't be able to read them.

It's not just the comedians. The left has simply gone nuts, even more than usual. Liberals would have us believe that it is because of Trump's policies or his character, but he's done nothing other than what he promised on immigration and many other issues. The real reason is they have lost power. They have lost the presidency after basking in Obama for eight years.

Are they seriously claiming that Trump is too crude for them — the left, the masters of vulgarity and the steadfast opponents of fixed moral standards? By what standard do they condemn Trump?

They say they abhor Trump because he disrespects women, yet they worship the most notorious womanizer of all time — Bill Clinton. Give me a break.

Yes, liberals would have us believe that they are highly respectful of women and that their respect transcends partisan politics. But for the left, nothing transcends party politics. Liberals like women, gays and ethnic minorities — except when they're conservative. Liberals routinely treat pro-life women as traitors to their gender. CBS News anchor Gayle King recently thanked Ivanka Trump for agreeing to an interview, calling her Mrs. Kushner — a faux pas she most likely would have been mortified over had someone on the right uttered it.

Leftists claim to be defenders of democracy, yet they assault the democratic process at every turn. They just refuse to accept the results of the presidential election. Their bureaucratic armies in federal agencies, from the Environmental Protection Agency to the Department of Labor, openly defy Trump's executive orders. Their appellate judges twist the law into pretzels to thwart his lawful orders on immigration and his travel ban. They take to the streets to commit criminal acts of violence disguised as lawful protests, vandalizing property and creating mayhem. They assault police officers in the name of protecting American workers — as if cops aren't American workers. They use violence to silence opposing political voices on the pretense that those opponents might incite violence. Their behavior is almost too absurd to take seriously — except it has very serious consequences, so we must showcase it.

Please, let them keep making jackasses of themselves so that the American people will see just how extreme the left has become — and will realize that this extremism has taken over the Democratic Party. Exposing liberals can only be in the best interests of this country.

If you think I'm exaggerating about the Democratic Party, you probably didn't hear Democratic National Chairman Tom Perez telling immigrant workers: "No human being is illegal. We must treat everyone with dignity. ... The Democratic Party will always be here, fighting for you."

What exactly does Perez mean by that last line? Does his party support immigration enforcement or not? This is radical stuff, folks.

But it's no worse than liberal media's ghastly behavior at the White House Correspondents' Association dinner. It's no worse than Democratic Rep. Maxine Waters' saying it's "absolutely racist" for Trump to be hard-nosed on immigration and saying Trump is a "disgusting, poor excuse of a man." It's no worse than Democratic Sen. Cory Booker's saying the GOP health care bill would "mean death" if it were to become law or than House Minority Leader Nancy Pelosi's saying the bill is "stupid," "a moral monstrosity that will devastate seniors" and "a very sad, deadly joke." It's no worse than Democratic CNN political commentator Paul Begala's calling Trump "a moral midget." It's no worse than "The Daily Show's" Hasan Minhaj calling Trump the "liar in chief." And it's no less vile than CNN's David Gregory's gender-baiting by partially blaming Hillary Clinton's loss on "misogyny."

The Democrats would have us believe they're the party of inclusion. That's rich, considering Perez's announcement that pro-life supporters are not welcome in the Democratic Party.

Democrats would have us believe they are the party of tolerance. That's also rich, considering King's asking Trump's chief economic adviser, Gary Cohn, "What's a nice registered Democrat boy doing working in a Republican administration?" There you go. You must not be nice if you work for Republicans.

Let them keep it up. Let them keep rioting, destroying property and hurting people in the name of love and harmony. Let them continue to suppress speech in the name of democracy. Let them demean and curse President Trump in the name of civility.

This is the very kind of childish insolence that led to the American people's rejecting them and electing Donald Trump in November. Please keep it up, ladies and gentlemen, and we'll just further build our coalition. America will be better off for it, and we thank you for that.

Past Time to End This
Democratic Witch Hunt

May 12, 2017

I don't deny that President Trump's firing of FBI Director James Comey was handled poorly, but it pales in comparison with the Democrats' ongoing partisan witch hunt against President Trump concerning Russia. That should be the story.

Shortly after Trump's dismissal of Comey, Trump defenders had plenty of ammunition. Widely respected and nonpartisan Deputy Attorney General Rod Rosenstein had reportedly recommended that Trump fire Comey.

But then the communications from Team Trump on the matter seemed to muddy the waters. Though maintaining that Rosenstein's recommendation was pivotal, Trump spokespeople added other reasons. They claimed that Trump had fired Comey based on his handling of the Hillary Clinton email investigation and because numerous FBI agents and employees were dispirited by Comey's actions.

Then acting FBI Director Andrew McCabe testified, "The vast majority of FBI employees enjoyed a deep, positive connection to Director Comey." A number of retired FBI officials also apparently showed solidarity with Comey by using his face for their Facebook profile photos. And though Rosenstein has contradicted mainstream media reports that he was contemplating resigning over the narrative that he had recommended Comey's dismissal, he reportedly claims that he did not expressly recommend the firing. Oh, boy.

Trump added more to the mix when he told Lester Holt in an interview that he had decided to fire Comey irrespective of the reported Rosenstein recommendation. Media outlets are having a field day with this alleged contradiction. Trump has thrown his communications team under the bus, they say, because his spokespeople clearly said that Trump's firing was a response to the recommendation. Trump's tweets concerning possible recorded conversations between him and Comey didn't help, either.

What a mess.

Though it doesn't look good that Trump's version arguably varies from that of his spokespeople, I don't see any major inconsistency here. I suspect that Trump was increasingly frustrated with Comey and wanted to fire him and that the recommendation helped justify it. Either way, Trump had the constitutional authority to fire Comey, and it would be scandalous only if he did so to impede a legitimate investigation into his alleged collusion with Russia, which is not the case.

Trump is obviously exasperated that the Democrats are impeding his policy agenda with their obsessive hammering of the bogus charge that he and his team conspired with Russia to interfere with the presidential election.

Despite the incessant media reports and congressional investigations, not a shred of evidence has emerged to substantiate the charge of collusion. We keep saying this, but the media and Democrats keep pretending otherwise. It's unconscionable. Even James Clapper, former President Barack Obama's director of national intelligence, has admitted that there is no evidence of collusion and that he has no reason to suspect it.

The real scandal is not Trump's firing Comey — even if Trump's supporters are unhappy with the timing and the way it was handled and communicated. The scandal is the liberal establishment's coordinated conspiracy to falsely allege that Trump stole the presidency by colluding with Russia. Liberals absolutely know that it's not true, but they will not quit bearing false witness. How dare they posture indignantly about Trump's supposed dishonesty?

The Democrats know they are fabricating this whole thing, but they figure this is the best way they can thwart Trump's efforts to move the country forward and out of the multiple quagmires Obama landed this country in. Their constant laments about the democratic process are laughably belied by their refusal to accept the results of the presidential election.

It is the Democrats' prerogative to act as the opposition party and to try to impede Trump's agenda. But it is reprehensible that they are doing so through fraudulent means and further dividing the country with their lies about Team Trump and Russia.

Their counterfeit hysteria knows no bounds. Not long ago, Democrats were demanding Comey's head, alleging that his public announcements had sabotaged Hillary Clinton's presidential campaign. Now they are claiming the firing is a "constitutional crisis" and a "coup." Not only did Trump have the authority to fire Comey but also the termination does not end the investigation.

Author Jon Meacham claimed on "Morning Joe" that Trump had removed someone "in charge of an investigation that could lead to treason." Sen. Richard Blumenthal said the firing may well lead to impeachment hearings. Senate Minority Leader Chuck Schumer called on the Justice Department to appoint a special prosecutor to oversee the FBI's investigation into the Trump campaign.

Hillary Clinton's 2016 running mate, Sen. Tim Kaine, said: "We have a deeply insecure president who understands that the noose is tightening because of this Russia investigation. And that's why I believe he has let Jim Comey go."

Kaine knows better. There is no evidence that there is any noose, much less that it's tightening, and the media's claim that Trump fired Comey because he was seeking more funds to investigate him has been expressly denied by acting Director McCabe. CNN's Van Jones said that the only people who are happy about the firing "are sitting in the Kremlin." MSNBC's Chris Matthews claimed that the firing was "a little whiff of fascism." Countless liberal media and political figures are comparing the Comey firing to the Saturday Night Massacre, in which Richard Nixon fired Watergate special prosecutor Archibald Cox.

The way this firing transpired is unfortunate, but we wouldn't be talking about this if Democrats and the media weren't lying every hour of every day about a nonexistent scandal. This bogus investigation should end forthwith, no matter who is heading it, because it is based on nothing but innuendo and partisanship. You conduct an investigation not because you want something to be true but because you have some evidence suggesting it may be. There is no such evidence here, and they've admitted it. Let's move on.

Defending Trump Against Excessive Charges Is Not Selling Out

May 19, 2017

One thing should be clear, at least to Republicans: The left has had the long knives out for President Donald Trump since before he was inaugurated. It intended to destroy him regardless of his conduct in office.

Liberals and even some conservatives contend that Trump's defenders on the right are tainted, partisan, idolatrous cheerleaders who have sold their souls and principles to defend him against troublesome charges. Some argue that even if former Presidents Barack Obama and Bill Clinton engaged in similar activities, two wrongs don't make a right.

Trump supporters, they say, have always insisted they are strict adherents of the rule of law but are showing their true colors in defending Trump. But are they? Why is defending Trump against these excessive charges a betrayal of the rule of law? Just because he's handled some things disappointingly doesn't mean he's committed a crime or an impeachable offense. The rule of law requires that we be discriminating about these matters and not jump on the bandwagon to condemn Trump just because we don't approve of some of his actions or statements.

Without question, the rule of law and all other principles must be given the highest priority, and the Trump presidency doesn't change that. But there's something more involved here than mere Democratic hypocrisy.

We are talking about Democratic and liberal media wrongdoing. Obama, when injecting himself into the investigation concerning

Hillary Clinton's emails and saying that no criminal activity had occurred, actually engaged in the very conduct of which Trump is being sloppily accused. The left had no objection. But at this point, it sure doesn't appear that Trump's comments to then-FBI Director James Comey about then-national security adviser Michael Flynn rose to the level of interfering with a proceeding, much less obstruction of justice.

Liberals are also engaged in wrongdoing by conducting this ceaseless witch hunt against Trump for alleged collusion with Russia to interfere with the presidential election when they know there is no evidence of any collusion. It is reprehensible that they are perpetuating this slander to delegitimize Trump and undermine the will of the American people.

So no, two wrongs don't make a right, but there aren't two equal "wrongs" here, and attempts to attribute moral equivalence to these separate sets of conduct are deceitful and scurrilous.

Of course, Trump supporters should not compromise their principles to defend him against legitimate charges, but we shouldn't throw him to the leftist wolves when the Democrats make false, excessive and otherwise unwarranted charges against him. There are a number of things I will criticize Trump for, but I am not going to accede to the Democrats' outrageously over-the-top characterization of these actions as criminal or impeachable just to appear fairer or nonpartisan.

I'm also not about to quit pointing out the monumentally worse behavior of the leftist media and Democratic Party just to avoid the undiscriminating claim that I am a Trump cheerleader.

We have to analyze whether Trump is culpable of those things of which he has been accused, but in no event should such accusations intimidate or deter us from condemning the left for making false charges and trying to wrongfully undermine Trump's presidency.

Put another way, I am not defending Trump because he is being attacked by the left. I am not attacking the left because I am trying to change the subject from legitimate allegations against Trump. If I defend Trump, it is because I believe he deserves defending, and if I criticize the left, it is because I believe it deserves criticism. I am not compromising my principles to attack the left for trying to smear

Trump and destroy this country. I am acting in accordance with my principles.

Sure, Trump shoots from the hip on Twitter and in some interviews, but he did this long before the election. The question isn't whether he says things we wish he wouldn't or commits gaffes. The issue that is before us — and will remain before us for as long as he's in office because the Democrats will see to it, irrespective of Trump's actions — is whether Trump engaged in serious misconduct on any of these things. So far, it appears he has not — from the firing of Comey to alleged collusion with Russia to the Comey memo to the alleged sharing of classified information with Russia. So why are some conservatives suggesting Trump just resign? It is neither prudent nor fair to rush to judgment. Let's be guided by the evidence rather than innuendo or some anti-Trump hysteria.

I admit I'm concerned about Trump's apparent flip-flop on Jerusalem, his seeming ambivalence about certain health care issues, the recent budget fiasco, the wall and confusion around tax reform. I just wish Trump would return forthwith to the agenda on which he was elected and the commitments he made to seeing it through.

I believe that if he would redouble his efforts to clarify his legislative priorities and present strong, viable proposals on all these issues and exercise leadership to advance them, he would unite a majority around him sufficient to pass them. As long as he rededicates himself to his campaign promises, his base will not abandon him, even with his occasional gaffes.

In the meantime, let's recognize that the left is at war with us and is relentless in pursuing it. We must fight back as hard as the left is attacking if we expect our ideas to prevail. And we can do that without compromising our principles, so let's get to work.

Pros and Cons of Trump's Budget and Cons of Dem Demagoguery

May 26, 2017

Demagoguery and propaganda are enemies of good governance, but nowhere is that more apparent than in the federal budget, on which Democrats are shameless and too many Republicans are feckless.

Sages from American history presciently predicted that our republic would be in jeopardy if voters acquired the power to vote themselves money from the public trough. The U.S. Constitution did not contemplate that the federal government and federal politicians would be able to secure their elective offices through legislative transfers of wealth, but the sordid practice has been with us for decades, and we are paying the price.

Politicians can safely argue, in general terms, that we must balance the budget, but when they dare to provide specifics, they face charges of heartlessness. Well, it used to be heartlessness. Now Democrats have sunk to further depths to describe Republican efforts to cut or even just reduce the rate of spending increases as hateful, mean-spirited and simply evil. Never mind that if we don't quit this recklessness, someday we'll witness a fiscal catastrophe that will devastate the very people Democrats are pretending to protect.

Some sanguine politicians and pundits through the years have glibly dismissed concerns over the explosive growth of the deficits and debt as hyperventilating. "We'll be fine. What's all the fuss?"

Sadly, these experts on everything except common sense fail to recognize that when you continue to ignore the main drivers of federal spending, eventually they are going to be virtually impossible to reform, and in the meantime, they will severely retard economic growth.

Liberals have an easy job. All they need to do is promise benefits and apply dishonest marketing strategies to paint themselves as caring and their opponents as ogres. They don't need to designate how those benefits will be funded, and they slam the so-called rich for not paying their fair share — an abominably false claim.

With health care, for example, they make insurance coverage the issue rather than affordable, accessible health care with maximum consumer choice over health care providers and insurance plans. This insurance coverage criterion is grossly misleading but effective at deceiving the public.

Our health care system under Obamacare is unsustainable, yet Democrats will not help reform it. Our federal fiscal condition is unsustainable, yet Democrats actively obstruct any real remedies.

President Obama didn't even try to balance the budget with any of his unrealistically optimistic projected budgets. He didn't even bother because he wasn't worried about the government's living within its means. He was focused on transferring wealth and using taxpayer money to fund a smorgasbord of leftist projects, from environmental boondoggles to dangerous Iranian nuclear deals.

President Trump's first budget, however, exposes fault lines throughout the political system, not just among Democrats. To his credit, Trump at least aspires to balance the budget within 10 years based on certain growth assumptions. He proposed substantial spending reductions (at least reductions in the rate of increase and some actual cuts — e.g., $1.4 trillion from Medicaid, $1.5 trillion from nondefense discretionary spending, $274 billion from certain welfare programs and some from Social Security disability) in certain areas that even some Republican politicians have previously been afraid to tackle, from the Environmental Protection Agency to the State Department, including welfare reform.

Democrats and liberal commentators didn't wait half a news cycle to descend on Trump with full-throated moral condemnation. House Minority Leader Nancy Pelosi said Trump's budget is "literally a killer" for the American people. The always winsome Hillary Clinton denounced the budget as "an unimaginable level of cruelty." MSNBC host Joe Scarborough said Trump's budget is "hateful" and people are "scared as hell." Where have you gone, Joe (DiMaggio)? MSNBC's Chris Matthews said the budget was written for "the wealthy people." Republican John McCain and sidekick Lindsey Graham piously pronounced the proposal DOA.

So plaudits for Trump for these relatively bold proposals. Regrettably, however, Trump did not include any provisions to reform Medicare or Social Security retirement benefits. This is no surprise, because Trump campaigned on protecting these entitlements. The current proposals for health care reform also cloud the issue in a way that can't yet be measured.

So here's where we are. Trump deserves serious credit for his proposed action on discretionary spending — credit because these necessary cuts are the very type that lend themselves to Democratic and media demagoguery. He also deserves credit for at least trying to balance the budget in the next decade. We need to call out demagogic leftist critics for fraudulently framing these efforts as cruel and for deliberately ignoring that we have a duty to rein in spending.

On the other hand, conservatives need to talk truth to Trump about the entitlements that his present budget fails to address. Admittedly, the Democrats' reaction to these proposed cuts in discretionary spending is just a foretaste of what they'd do if Trump were to propose reforming entitlements. Regardless, if Trump wants to make a long-term impact on America's fiscal stability, he must address entitlements within the next few years.

With that caveat, I'm praising Trump for the good-faith incremental steps he's taken with this budget. Let's give praise where it's due and constructively criticize when appropriate.

Hillary Clinton — Endless Sore Loser

June 2, 2017

Attacks on President Donald Trump are commonplace — many depict him as this wildly bizarre, classless person occupying the Oval Office — but have critics fairly considered what a horror show a Hillary Clinton presidency would have been?

Why is this relevant, you ask? Well, because the liberal media are permanently afflicted with Trump derangement syndrome and won't quit feeding Clinton's narcissistic obsession with her defeat. Did the media fixate on Mitt Romney's defeat to Barack Obama and forever question him about it?

Clinton has been muttering about her loss since she recovered from the initial election-night shock, and it has been ugly. In early April — and probably earlier — she attributed her loss, in part, to misogyny. "It is fair to say ... certainly, misogyny played a role," she lamented at the Women in the World Summit in New York. "I mean, that just has to be admitted. ... Some people, women included, had real problems" with "the first woman president."

In early May, Clinton said she takes "personal responsibility" but then quickly contradicted herself by shifting blame to Russian interference in the election and then-FBI Director James Comey's release of a letter concerning the investigation into her emails.

Late in May, Clinton resurfaced at the Code Conference, denying she or her organization made any significant mistakes in the campaign and blaming many others and other factors for her loss. She said the Russian government orchestrated a vast disinformation campaign to discredit her, and she also blamed WikiLeaks' release of campaign chairman John Podesta's emails and speculated that

Trump had colluded with Russians to disseminate this information. She lambasted the media for covering her email chicanery as if it were Pearl Harbor, calling it "the biggest nothingburger ever." And for good measure, she further blamed sexism, saying that criticism of her six-figure speeches to various groups was gender-driven.

She introduced a new twist, however, in pointing her finger at her formerly beloved Democratic Party. "I get the nomination. ... I inherit nothing from the Democratic Party," she huffed. The Democratic National Committee "was bankrupt. It was on the verge of insolvency. Its data was mediocre to poor, nonexistent, wrong," she continued. "I had to inject money into it to keep it going." She also threw her fellow Democrats under the bus, saying that they "are not good historically at building institutions," adding, "We've got to get a lot better." Clinton said her campaign was further crippled by the widespread assumption that she was going to win.

Her attack on the DNC won her no friends in the party. Andrew Therriault, former data science director for the DNC, tweeted (and later deleted) profanity at Clinton's convenient narrative: "DNC data folks: today's accusations are f—-ing bull——, and I hope you understand the good you did despite that nonsense." He added, "Private mode be damned, this is too important. I'm not willing to let my people be thrown under the bus without a fight."

Nor did her attacks on the media sit well with certain media mavens. MSNBC host Andrea Mitchell said Clinton's claim that Americans colluded with Russia to "weaponize information" against her is "drawing a conspiracy theory" against the Trump campaign without evidence.

Isn't it interesting that it took an insult from Clinton to get a liberal media person to admit there's no evidence of Trump collusion with Russia?

Clinton's right about one thing: The Democratic Party is to blame. That's because it nominated her to run for president and even colluded with her against Bernie Sanders to ensure it happened.

But the main takeaway from Clinton's pathetically endless election post-mortem is that while Trump critics dwell on his alleged instability and lack of class, Clinton has further proved herself to be worse in reality than Trump is perceived to be.

I'm not talking about policy matters, albeit Clinton would have been an unspeakable disaster in that realm as president, too. I mean on a personal level, where this woman who has held herself out as a public servant all these years is a self-absorbed political animal and shows little grace and even less class. I have no doubt that the stories we've read about how she mistreats people are true.

Cursory inspection of her many scapegoats reveals that even if any of her claims have merit, she is the primary reason for every one of them. She was the virtual head of the DNC she castigates. Her own gross negligence (and criminality, truth be told) led to the FBI investigation, without which Comey wouldn't have made any statement. She bought into and perpetuated the narrative that she was the prohibitive favorite in the campaign. She offered no change from, much less any explanation for, Obama's horrendous record. Her campaign platform was simply, "Never Trump." She arrogantly refused to campaign in Wisconsin, a blue state that ultimately swung to Trump, and she didn't devote nearly enough resources to the other blue states of Michigan and Pennsylvania. She invites attention to gender in constantly whining about it on the one hand while lecturing us for considering it on the other. And can we all just please admit that she forfeited standing to complain about mistreatment of women long ago when she enabled her world-class womanizing husband's serially decadent dalliances? Despite her reputation for brilliance and experience, she couldn't defeat political novice Donald Trump in their debates.

Hillary Clinton was a disastrous candidate and would have been a worse president. How long must we endure these public postelection couch sessions?

Trump Won, Comey Minus One

June 9, 2017

Trying to be objective — and that's sometimes difficult for me when it comes to politics — I don't agree that former FBI Director James Comey's congressional testimony was equally good news and bad news for President Trump. Trump came away a decisive winner.

Most agree that Trump benefited from Comey's admission that Trump was not in fact under FBI investigation for colluding with the Russians or for anything else. But many Trump critics, left and right, see Comey's negative portrait of Trump as so damaging as to cancel out the positive news, which, on reflection, is incorrect.

It's true that Comey painted Trump as dishonest, petty and vindictive and as one who operates in office as a business executive rather than someone who respects the parameters of his authority. Even if true, is this caricature news to anyone? Trump's critics already believe it, and most of his supporters believe it is overstated.

This is not to say that Trump's defenders would approve of any abuses of authority, but they aren't predisposed to assume that every unorthodox action on Trump's part is malicious or indicative of a tyrannical or criminal mindset.

So the only "news" that emerged from Comey's testimony — the only facts that might change the status quo ante — was that Trump has not been under investigation this whole time. Not only that but he did not pressure or even attempt to persuade Comey to go softly on any of his associates on the Russia investigation if it were discovered they had some illicit interaction with the Russians.

For some, Comey landed a blow against Trump in alleging he told Comey he "hoped" the investigation against Flynn would end and in requesting from Comey "honest loyalty." Here again, Trump's attackers are predisposed to assume Trump was using code to direct Comey to stop investigating Flynn and to pledge his loyalty to Trump above his professional duties. Trump's defenders reject that, so on this issue, the needle didn't move a centimeter in either direction.

Some might say: "Hold on. This isn't just a matter of Trump supporters believing one way and his defenders another. Comey was the only one in the room, and he took Trump's words as directives."

Well, even if you assume that's what Trump meant, which I don't, legal experts agree that no one has been charged with obstruction of justice on such vague language as "hope." The thought of it is preposterous. Moreover, some experts argue that as chief executive, he has the power to end investigations conducted by the executive branch. Let's remember that the Flynn investigation and Russia investigation are two different matters and that Trump is not the target of either one of them. If it occurred, it would have been inappropriate behavior but hardly criminal or impeachable conduct.

But I don't believe that Comey's inferences are accurate. Trump is an advocate by nature and is loyal to his friends. It's perfectly reasonable to assume that he was just expressing his vote of confidence in Flynn's character and was by no means suggesting that Comey ignore hard evidence against him, much less directing him to.

I have a hard time believing that Comey really thought at the time that Trump was giving him orders. If he really believed so, then it is indisputable that he acted improperly at the time and thereafter. If he really believed Trump was trying to obstruct justice, he had a duty to do something about it, but instead, he decided to hold it close to the vest and only use it if he needed it later. Is that the way a man in his position should have behaved?

As to Trump's firing of Comey, if you were Trump, wouldn't you be outraged if Comey refused to disclose that you were not under investigation when everything else was leaked — as Sen. Marco Rubio noted? Didn't Trump have a right to be indignant over the lies being disseminated every day on this and a right to want to quell these lies that were impeding his agenda? Was it unreasonable for Trump to think Comey was biased against him, seeing as Comey refused to set the record straight on this matter when he'd certainly tried to set the record straight publicly on other issues before?

What about Comey's revelations concerning his own bizarre behavior? I was originally willing to believe that Comey was scrupulously aboveboard and would strive for objectivity — that he would try not to allow his personal biases to color his objectivity or influence the course of the investigation or his assessment of the evidence. Based on his own testimony, I am now quite skeptical.

Comey bent over backward to conclude that Hillary Clinton had no criminal intent in the handling of her private emails — yet his conclusion was in direct conflict with the evidence he meticulously detailed against her. It is hard to believe he would have given any other target such an enormous benefit of the doubt.

Yet despite his professed reluctance to infer criminal intent there, he leaped to such conclusions against Trump with the eagerness of a never-Trumper. "Hope" equals "You are hereby ordered"? Give me a break. "Loyalty" equals "I order you not to follow the evidence wherever it may lead you"? Come on now. These inferences wouldn't be reasonable for any investigator, but for Comey, who expressed reluctance to making inferences on intent, they are outrageous.

Comey damningly admitted he leaked information to a Columbia law professor in the hope that it would lead to the appointment of a special investigator. Some say Comey was within his rights as a private citizen. But as certain legal experts have noted, he acquired that information when he was working for the government, and it wasn't his private property. Comey holds himself out as the pinnacle of decorum but became a perpetrator of the very type of conduct he was self-righteously investigating.

Some applauded Comey's willingness to speak truth to power, but he admitted that he didn't object to Trump's allegedly improper overtures to him. In this hearing, Comey showed himself to be far too concerned with the public's perception about him and allowed his personal feelings and biases to interfere with his objectivity. In the end, he didn't lay a glove on Trump but significantly damaged himself — and, as a bonus, exposed Barack Obama's second attorney general, Loretta Lynch, as a perpetrator of the very behavior others have improperly attributed to Trump.

Leftist Extremism Is Mainstream Leftism
June 16, 2017

Just in case you think the political left has become more rational or less extreme, I refer you to the following examples demonstrating otherwise.

Some will say these are extreme cases, not representative of mainstream leftist (excuse the oxymoron) thought and practice, but we see such examples all the time — not to mention that this type of thinking is mainstreamed in the liberal media and academia. Others will dispute that these are examples of wrongheaded thinking, which will prove that I'm not overstating my case.

Item: In her high-school graduation speech in Pennsylvania, Moriah Bridges was prohibited from praying blessings on her class; she was barred from thanking her "Heavenly Father" and her "Lord." The school's principal, at the direction of the school district, said her prepared remarks would have been unconstitutional. Folks, the courts have stretched the federal and state establishment clauses to absurd lengths to say that almost any expression of Christianity at a government-supported entity is prohibited. How can anyone reasonably argue that to allow a student to voluntarily offer a public prayer constitutes government support of Christianity? Does anyone ever consider the First Amendment's free exercise clause, which precedes the establishment clause? Both clauses are designed to promote, not suppress, religious liberty, yet this school district's Christian-hostile action in fact suppressed Bridges' religious liberty in the name of protecting that very freedom.

Item: Along the same lines, Bremerton High School football coach Joe Kennedy was fired for refusing to comply with the

Washington state school's order that he quit praying silently on the field because it was an impermissible public display of religion by a public school employee. Such prayer, according to the school, could be interpreted as the school district's endorsement of religion. See what I mean? Kennedy is challenging this in court.

Item: Vero Beach High School student J.P. Krause was initially disqualified from winning his election as class president because he used tongue-in-cheek campaign slogans mirroring President Trump's campaign rhetoric on the proposed border wall. Krause's frivolous suggestion that they build a wall between their school and a rival school and make the other school pay for it was deemed insulting and harassment under the school district's rules, according to the school's principal. This is so self-evidently absurd as to obviate further comment. Only after public outcry did the Florida school's superintendent reverse the principal's decision.

Item: You know how same-sex marriage advocates tell us that they just want equal rights — that they just want everyone to live and let live? Transgender activist blogger Tiffany Berruti stated that if a person isn't attracted to transgender people, he or she is "deeply transphobic." So it is transphobic to ask or demand that a transgender person identify himself, herself or themselves as being transgender? There are just no words. If you think there are, then you may be making my case for me.

Item: Evergreen State College established a "Day of Absence" event, in which white community members were urged to leave campus for a day, as reported by Fox News' Tucker Carlson. Professor Bret Weinstein questioned the idea and was confronted by some 50 students, who demanded he resign, and some members of the Evergreen community mocked or maligned him. Weinstein held a class off campus because university police informed him it was not safe for him to be on campus. "They imagine that I am a racist and that I am teaching racism in the classroom," said Weinstein. "And that has caused them to imagine that I have no right to speak and that I am harming students by the very act of teaching them." Do people not understand that setting aside a day to discourage whites from campus promotes racism — encouraging people to see people stereotypically, as members of a race, rather than as individuals? And if some acts of racism did occur on this campus, isn't it racist to punish an entire group (white people) based on the behavior of a few? This is stunningly absurd.

Item: A LendEDU poll of 1,659 U.S. college students shows that 36 percent of them think "safe spaces" are "absolutely necessary" on campus, while only 37 percent disagree. Safe spaces are places adults can go where no one will hurt their feelings. For example, female student government officers at Barnard College sponsored a safe space event offering hot chocolate and "feminist coloring pages" when Donald Trump was elected president. Again, I'll not insult your intelligence by assuming you need me to comment on this lunacy.

Item: Liberals, from Congress to "The View," cried that President Trump's calling members of the Islamic State group "losers" was irresponsible and could lead to terrorist recruitment and further terrorist attacks. These people would prefer that we use gentle language to describe their heinous murders because we don't want to offend and incite other people. You know, otherwise civil people could be so outraged that they might turn into murderous losers themselves. Who thinks like this? Well, a frightening number of people on the left, that's who. And if you don't believe that, then you're simply not paying attention.

As you very well know, I could go on and on. But deniers would still say I'm generalizing. Others need hot chocolate and coloring pages. Still others would defend the examples. And that should speak for itself.

Democratic Party More
Bankrupt Than Ever

June 23, 2017

The Democrats' comprehensive meltdown after their fifth straight election loss is a spectacle worth savoring. They're vacillating between denial and self-flagellation, between consuming depression and delusional optimism. Some are even blaming hacking for the loss.

Don't let them fool you; they did not expect carpetbagger Jon Ossoff to lose to Karen Handel in the special election for Georgia's 6th Congressional District. If they had, they would not have poured unprecedented millions into the race. No one but gambling addicts intentionally waste that kind of money.

For all the talk about President Donald Trump's being in trouble, the Democratic Party is on the ropes. Democrats are in the minority in the federal and state legislative branches, and they've now sustained five consecutive losses in special House elections. The Federal Election Commission reports that the Democratic National Committee raised only $4.3 million in May — the worst May for fundraising since 2003. April efforts were almost as dismal.

I can't remember the last time I heard Democrats beating themselves up this intensely and openly. "Our brand is worse than Trump," Rep. Tim Ryan, D-Ohio, said. "We can't just run against Trump." Ouch. Other Democratic leaders are signaling signs of mutiny against House Minority Leader Nancy Pelosi.

On the other hand, some Democrats insist these losses are a portent of great things to come. Former Sen. Barbara Boxer says Democrats will do fine in 2018. Likewise, Democratic

Congressional Campaign Committee Chairman Ben Ray Lujan says, "The House is in play (in 2018)." He wrote, "I don't make this statement lightly — I've never said it before. ... This is about much more than one race."

But, Rep. Lujan, there hasn't been just one race; there've been five. If Democrats actually have unprecedented grass-roots energy and impressive candidates but still can't win, what does that say about your party's predicament?

Then again, Democrats can't even agree whether Ossoff was a good candidate. They expressed no doubts before the election, especially not to their witless Hollywood sugar daddies when soliciting funds for this mega-hyped wunderkind.

The Democrats' problem is that they are intellectually and morally bankrupt, as I argued in my 2006 book, "Bankrupt." It's not that they don't have policy ideas. It's that their ideas don't work, so they just attack and demonize Republicans. Though Trump is often a convenient target, they would (and did) crucify any Republican president in office. And despite the leftward cultural shift of the nation and their virtual monopoly on academia, the mainstream media and Hollywood, their polices are not that popular with the American people, so they can't afford to be completely honest about them.

Ossoff, for example, was hardly running as a liberal. Why would liberals tout a candidate who wasn't running as a liberal unless they knew he was pretending? More importantly, why would this darling of the left have run as a moderate — unless he and his party knew he wouldn't have stood a chance had he run as a liberal Democrat?

The truth is not the Democrats' friend. They are engaging in stunning deceit over President Trump's alleged collusion with Russia and claims that he obstructed an investigation. Not only was there no obstruction but also Trump had no incentive to obstruct an investigation into something that didn't occur.

Even the Democrats' feigned outrage over Russian "interference with our democracy" is a sham. It would be one thing if the Russians had disseminated lies about Hillary Clinton, but instead they exposed damaging truths about her. Without defending Russian perfidy, did that actually hurt the democratic process in the sense of informing voters? What does harm the democratic process is the Democrats' assault on the integrity of the voting process, from blocking voter ID laws to facilitating the voting of immigrants who are here illegally. And if Democrats were so committed to the democratic process, they would quit trying to nullify the will of the people with manufactured Hail Mary impeachment attempts.

Truth be told, nothing would hurt the Democrats more than an authentic referendum on their policy agenda — a legitimate unfolding of the democratic process they profess to treasure. Knowing this, they do everything they can to make elections about anything but their policies.

They know, for instance, that Obamacare is a failure and a poster child for failed liberal policies. Yet as premiums and deductibles skyrocket and choice and quality of care plummet, they barely concede that it is problematic. Their "policy" argument is to say Republicans want to hurt and kill Americans by repealing and replacing their abominable plan. On taxes, immigration and other policies, we are simply mean-spirited bigots. These tired lies are all they have.

But the Democratic establishment is nothing if not arrogant and unimaginative. Though focus groups and elections reveal that even Democratic voters are sick of these bottomless and unfruitful Russian investigations, they are going to keep beating this dead horse, hoping it comes to life.

Democrats are welcome to fool themselves into believing they've dealt Trump a deathblow, but his approval ratings aren't much lower than when he took office — despite their endless slandering. They have nothing new against Trump. They are just recycling the criticisms they made during the election campaign, which he won.

Let the Democrats keep hallucinating and dissembling. Let them keep lying about Trump — because with every passing day, their bankruptcy is more apparent. But in the meantime, pray that President Trump will resist the temptation to be distracted by these sordid Democratic efforts to undermine our democracy. Instead of focusing too much energy on defending himself, he needs to reignite a fire under the American people — and particularly Republicans — to move forward with his agenda. This week, with his uplifting speech in Iowa and the Senate's rollout of a health care bill, could be a promising reboot.

Mark Levin's
'Rediscovering Americanism'

June 30, 2017

My friend Mark Levin is nothing if not a patriot of the first order. He loves the United States and its founding principles — and his latest book, "Rediscovering Americanism," explains his passion and encourages ours.

Levin believes that America's greatness lies in its unique founding ideals and correctly observes — and documents — how far we've strayed from those principles and the structure of government they inspired.

In his other books, Levin has outlined the problems confronting us and proposed solutions, but in this book, he takes a deeper look into the Framers' vision and examines the anatomy and historical development of the pernicious progressive mindset that has systematically chipped away at our governmental structure and our liberties.

This book is remarkable in its simultaneous succinctness and thoroughness. It's hard to fathom how Levin could have adeptly covered so much important, relevant material in a relatively short book. But he did.

Why would Levin take us on this historical tour of our nation's competing political and philosophical ideas? Haven't we moved beyond such considerations in the modern age, with the federal government micromanaging so many aspects of our lives? Do these lofty notions even matter anymore in our modern era of short attention spans, sound bites and our endless obsession with daily polling? Why contemplate the proper role of government when our ruling class rarely concerns itself with preserving our liberties, when the Washington establishment rarely focuses on whether government has the authority to act but fights instead over the most efficient way it should act?

The answer is that Levin understands that our belief and confidence in our founding principles and our steadfast commitment to them are essential to preserving our individual liberties, our prosperity and our national uniqueness and greatness. In Levin's words, "philosophy and practical politics are linked and, therefore, have a real effect on the life of the individual." As our history has increasingly demonstrated, we cannot preserve our constitutional structure — and thus our liberties and the rest — if we do not understand and embrace its necessity. For our failure to grasp that truth has resulted in the steady erosion of the system built on it.

Levin is convinced that unless we have a national reawakening of the indispensability of our first principles, we will continue our march toward statism and squander the blessings bestowed on us by our visionary ancestors. "What will (future generations) say about us?" he asks. "Will they say that we were a wise and conscientious people who understood and appreciated the blessings of our existence and surroundings and prudentially and conscientiously cared for them; or will they say we were a self-indulgent and inattentive people, easily shepherded in one direction or another, who stole the future from our own children and generations yet born, and squandered an irreplaceable heritage?"

In other words, our remarkable system of government, despite its brilliance, is not self-sustaining. An intellectually lazy and spiritually negligent body politic will not nurture and care for this gift, and it will continue to descend by incremental steps into tyranny beyond the point of redemption.

By reintroducing us to our founding ideas and their importance, Levin is both sounding an alarm over the threats that imperil us and calling on us to man our battle stations by first understanding the gravity of our predicament and then arming ourselves with a true understanding of our national uniqueness.

In Chapter 1, Levin unpacks the concept of natural law (and natural rights) — "the foundational principle at the core of American society." This principle "permeated American thought from the beginning of our republic and well before."

As clearly and firmly reflected in the Declaration of Independence, all men are created equal by God and have certain unalienable rights. These rights are universal to all men and are divine and spiritual in origin — not government constructs — and thus no government has the right to deny them. Levin shows further the importance of the rule of law, the mutual dependence between private property and freedom, and the interrelationship between economic liberty and political liberty.

The Framers designed our system to preserve these rights (and liberties), thus crafting a constitution that empowered and limited government — with those powers and limitations each designed to achieve the overarching goal of establishing and preserving our individual liberties. The Framers understood that mankind is imperfect and that a government led by imperfect people would, unless checked, tyrannize citizens and swallow their liberties.

Progressives, on the other hand, believe that mankind is perfectible and that centralized government is the means to achieving this social engineering, and they have been working steadily toward that goal in America for more than a century.

Whereas our Framers ardently believed that mankind's natural rights are transcendent and that the principles they enshrined in the Constitution are also timeless, progressives have always been convinced that our founding principles and documents were applicable only to their unique historical setting and that our system must constantly evolve to accommodate the changing times.

The tragic irony is that our short national history has vindicated the Framers and exposed the folly of the progressives, who are still in denial that their arrogant attempts to engineer human perfection through expansive government — particularly the runaway administrative state — have resulted in a stunning erosion of our liberties.

Unless we dismantle the federal leviathan and its suffocating bureaucracy, we'll slide ever further — and irreversibly — into tyranny. Unless we "rediscover" our "Americanism," we can't conceivably resurrect and sustain our liberties.

Read this book and rediscover.

The Ongoing Frustration of Trump's Conservative Critics

July 7, 2017

The frustration of many Trump critics on the right, or MTCRs, is palpable and growing. Some are becoming more elitist by the day and utterly out of touch with rank-and-file conservatives, which is a particularly bitter pill to swallow because they believe they are the main arbiters of what conservatism means.

Some are obviously disgusted with everything about Trump — his demeanor, his tweets, his combativeness, his bigger-than-life personality, his egotism and tons more. Their revulsion blinds them to anything positive. They are so invested in Trump's failure that they can't stomach rooting for him even when he's advancing conservative policies or fighting those dedicated to obstructing them. Their unhealthy Trump obsession compels them to present evidence every passing hour to justify their opposition.

I've seen their ire and experienced their snobbish condemnation on social media. It has become personal for many because they apparently view conservative Trump supporters as frauds and sellouts. They attack our character instead of considering that our calculus is that Trump may advance a conservative agenda more successfully than presidents ostensibly more conservative than he.

What MTCRs don't seem to grasp is that rank-and-file conservatives largely support Trump. They aren't mortified by his every tweet. They refuse to allow the perfect to be the enemy of the good.

Most Trump supporters are not cultists who are blind and indifferent to his faults and indelicacies, but nor are they soiling themselves in agony over them. They have not betrayed their principles in supporting and defending Trump. They are not hypocrites for cheering him on against the plethora of leftist assaults. They don't root for Trump because they seek revenge against the left, as some have wrongly supposed. The left's war on America, as founded, is ongoing, not some one-off offense for which we seek redress.

Trump supporters see a bigger picture here — greater stakes, bigger hills to die on. They support him as the last best hope to save America — or at least to return it to the right path. They're behind him because they believe he is attempting to turn the country around and, in many cases, succeeding. They are ecstatic that he is standing up to the political left and firing back — so they aren't going to be overly exercised over his every fault. He is filling the enormous void in Washington created by feckless politicians and commentators on the right who have refused to show the will to strike back against the left.

Rank-and-file conservatives are convinced that America and Western civilization are imperiled. They understand the damage done to our founding principles, values, traditions and mores and the harm inflicted on the Constitution and rule of law by generations of leftist assaults.

For them, politics is not a Beltway parlor game or a matter of petty partisanship. It's about saving the nation for themselves and their children. They see the urgency, and no amount of highhanded judgmentalism from smug conservative elites about their alleged hyperbole and hysteria is going to shame them into denial.

When parents in this country refuse to specify their newborn babies' gender on their birth certificates, we know that postmodernism and moral relativism have made their marks. We recognize intellectual and moral anarchy. Dismiss this as anecdotal irrelevancy if you will, but honest observers of the American scene witness such absurdity every day. Our culture is rife with it — from our universities to Hollywood to the media.

Some of the most indignant MTCRs cautioned restraint in criticizing President Obama, telling us either that we were exaggerating the horrors of his crusade to radically transform

America as founded or that our opposition would backfire. They were pragmatic, and we were dogmatic and reactionary.

Ironically, their pragmatism contributed to the frustration that culminated in the Trump movement. Yet now these self-appointed arbiters of genuine conservatism are accusing conservative Trump supporters, whom they formerly criticized for being conservative extremists, of abandoning conservatism. It seems that MTCRs are dwindling in numbers, but the most ardent ones are still oblivious to the Trump phenomenon and why it originated.

But what about Trump's tweets? Well, most conservatives aren't bothered by most of Trump's tweets, because they are just a continuation of what Trump was doing in plain sight during the primaries. Not every supporter approves of every tweet, but I dare say they love that Trump is finally taking the fight to the leftist media and putting them back on their heels for the first time in our adult lifetimes — again, not for revenge but because the leftist media are enemies of truth and must be confronted.

Besides, why should we become humorless boors like some of our brethren on the left? Let's not take ourselves so seriously that we feign outrage over tweets that not only don't foster violence as alleged but parody it. We've been waiting for someone to feed the left some of its own medicine. That moment has arrived. Enjoy it.

MTCRs are indignant that Trump supporters point to leftist hypocrisy and malfeasance when debating the propriety of Trump's media-lampooning tweets. But conservatives have always criticized the left. Would they have us declare a moratorium on opposition to liberalism to avoid any appearance of condoning Trump? Sorry, but we will not unilaterally disarm for fear of being accused of hypocrisy.

Moreover, it is ludicrous to suggest that Trump threatens the free press merely because he is fighting back. These are powerful entities dedicated not to the reporting of news but to hiding behind the First Amendment to destroy him personally and to delegitimize his presidency and thwart his agenda, at the expense of doing their job of reporting the news.

Another irony is that if MTCRs would quit obsessing over Trump instead of his policy agenda, they might have a better chance of influencing him in a conservative direction on issues where it could make a difference, such as in health care and tax reform. But for now, their knee-jerk aversion to Trump has rendered them impotent.

Of course, Trump doesn't deserve a pass from conservative criticism when it's warranted. But let's not lose our heads and criticize him out of pride or bitterness — and let's try to stay focused on issues that truly matter.

Retaining Our Principles Includes Keeping Our Eyes on the Big Ball

July 14, 2017

Amid the endless media obsession with Trump scandal allegations, important policy issues are getting short shrift. Considering that the left is happy with the status quo — the autopilot advancement of statism — this can only please Democrats.

Based on the overwhelming trend of national and state elections since 2010, the nation now firmly rejects liberal policies. Whether or not Democrats get the message, they don't intend to move right to accommodate the electorate.

Rather, they will continue undermining the will of the people through the courts, administrative agencies, Obama executive staff holdovers opposing voter ID laws, and a perpetual motion narrative against President Trump involving scandalmongering, character assassination and ongoing demonization of conservatives. Given their assault on democratic processes, it's hard to take serious their professed anxiety over election interference.

Regardless of the merits of current claims against Trump, the Democrats planned to delegitimize him the second he won the election. Allegations of collusion with the Russians to influence our election were based on shards of half-truths designed to appear incriminating but ultimately lacking a credible evidentiary basis.

You might object, "Well, with the latest bombshells concerning Donald Trump Jr.'s illicit meeting with a Russian lawyer, we can see that Trump's accusers were right all along." Not so fast.

Apart from whether it was wrong or inappropriate for Trump Jr. to take the meeting, there is still no evidence of actual collusion or, I would argue, even so-called attempted collusion. We can't possibly know what he would have done with that information had it been forthcoming, because we don't know — and he doesn't know — what that information was supposed to be, much less what it was.

To collude, you have to collude to do something. By attending the meeting to hear the lawyer out, what was Trump colluding to do other than hear her out? Information may yet be uncovered that damages team Trump, but until then, while this story gives Trump critics juicy ammo and makes many uncomfortable, it does not vindicate nefarious Democratic efforts to destroy Trump since the beginning.

My purpose here is not to litigate Trump Jr.'s meeting. It is to underscore that Democrats have not been in good faith in their witch hunt against Trump, and that their actions are having devastating consequences on the nation. Let's not forget that former FBI Director James Comey informed them privately that Trump was not under investigation for collusion with Russia, and they nevertheless misrepresented to the public that Trump was the primary target.

Moreover, those operating under the illusion that the Democrats' misbehavior is only about Trump would do well to remember their unconscionable behavior toward President George W. Bush. It wouldn't matter if Mother Teresa were president; Democrats would still be scandalmongering.

So, let's not be deterred from fighting Democrats for fear of being accused by Trump opponents on both sides of the aisle of "whataboutism" — diverting attention from alleged Trump scandals by blaming Democrats of similar misconduct. Don't worry. Any scandal allegations will be investigated and reported ad nauseam, so it would take more than a few spin doctors to pull that off.

No, diversion and rationalization are not my aims. I'm concerned about moving the nation back in the right direction, and that necessitates understanding the goals and tactics of the Democrats, who are pulling out all the stops to prevent such remedial action.

So, could we please recognize what we're up against and get in this fight instead of naval-gazing and always sprinting to assume the worst of those on our side? Could we, in the words of my colorful torts professor, keep our eyes on the big ball, even as we evaluate scandal allegations? The left wants to consummate its plan —

greatly accelerated by President Obama — to fundamentally transform American into something the Framers wouldn't recognize.

Relative to that, have you seen Sen. Bernie Sanders' hysterical tirades about Republican policies? And no, Sanders is not merely some quirky extremist who's unrepresentative of the Democratic Party. This character might have won the Democratic nomination but for Democratic National Committee *collusion* with Hillary Clinton.

Referring to Trump, Sanders said: "It's not just temperament, and it's not just his stupid tweets. Do not forget for a second that the policies that he is proposing are the most destructive policies being proposed in our lifetimes. This legislation that he is urging Congress to pass would throw 23 million Americans off of health insurance." He later added that up to 28,000 Americans could die each year — "nine times more than the tragic losses we suffered on 9/11, every single year."

Right, Bernie, we are going to kill people by allowing them the freedom to not buy health insurance and by introducing market forces to improve access to *affordable* health care — not just health insurance coverage.

Democrats have accused Republicans of pushing grandma off the cliff for years. In their view, though they'll never say it directly, capitalism is heartless because it caters only to the rich. They'll play the good-intentions-despite-bad-results card as long as they're breathing, but a rudimentary knowledge of history reveals their stunning ignorance. You don't have to be Milton Friedman to understand that socialism is the world's greatest generator of poverty. Oh, how I wish we had better messaging and more confidence in the power of our ideas to counter their revisionism.

So, while I don't deny that President Trump sometimes gives Democrats and the media fodder they can use to try to attack him, and thus, any advancement of conservative policies, they will vilify any Republican who proposes legislation and lawful executive action aimed at even slightly retarding the socialist juggernaut as extremist — and when it comes to policy, Trump is hardly an ideological extremist.

Why else do you think Democrats like Sen. Elizabeth Warren, believed by many to be a potential presidential contender, rally their radical acolytes through calls of "resistance"? They are hell-bent on resisting any effort to put the breaks on their tyranny.

So, no matter how much some of you dislike Trump or believe he just won't do, please don't get so preoccupied that you lose sight of the stakes. No, we must never abandon our principles or excuse any misconduct from our side. But my principles preclude a knee-jerk willingness to pile on Trump when unwarranted, and they include a steady focus on the gravity of what we're fighting for, as well as an unvarnished awareness that those we're fighting against are tireless, relentless and ruthlessly unscrupulous.

OK, GOP: No More Excuses!

July 21, 2017

Until now, I haven't been too concerned about the Republican Party's difficulties in passing a health care reform bill because delays have resulted in improvements to the proposed legislation. But enough is enough. No more games.

It's time to quit the finger-pointing. Neither congressional leaders nor President Trump have done enough to whip votes and sell the bill.

A major overhaul of Obamacare, whether a full repeal, or a repeal and replacement, is imperative for Trump and congressional Republicans. More than any other, Obamacare is the issue that has galvanized grass-roots conservatives since 2010, and the Republicans' failure to act now will be devastating on multiple levels.

Excuses like "we had a few renegade senators on the left and the right" won't work. Then-President Obama had no problem getting a majority to support Obamacare and was even able, albeit through deceit and legislative bribery, to cobble together a filibuster-proof margin.

So why can't Republicans get their act together? The differences are that Obama wanted this more than anything else and thus almost willed it into existence, and Democrats are far more monolithic than Republicans and stick together. Republicans must show the same fierce determination Obama showed when he crammed his monstrosity down our throats.

This requires a concerted team effort. President Trump must focus far more attention on this than he has, and his meetings with

Senate Republicans this week were a good start. For now, congressional Republicans must also make this their highest priority. Once the bill passes, Trump and Republican legislators must move on to tax reform with the same unified focus and determination.

Like never before, Trump must use the full extent of his political capital to sell the public on this bill and pressure recalcitrant legislators. He should hold major rallies in the states whose senators are balking, and give substantive speeches on what is at stake and why this bill is the lynchpin to reversing Obama's agenda. For their part, congressional Republicans need to be all over television and flood print media with op-eds pushing this bill.

Both Trump and GOP legislators must detail how Obamacare is failing and underscore the failed promises Obama made to advance this bill. In the process, they must change the narrative to distinguish between health care insurance (a term that has been bastardized, anyway) and affordable, quality health care with maximum consumer choices. For far too long, Democrats have corrupted the national conversation by fearmongering and distorting the English language.

I don't deny that the current version of the Senate bill is far from ideal from a conservative point of view, but it is far better than it was before, and it is light-years better than the status quo. I confess that I have been torn on supporting measures that many believe are Obamacare Lite, but in the end, we have to do the best we can do and go forward. We cannot let the perfect be the enemy of the good.

I think we have a far better chance of passing a so-called repeal-and-replace bill, which could be more accurately described as a partial repeal and replacement than a full-blown repeal. Either way, one must occur without further delay.

Many pundits assume that if left alone, Obamacare will continue to unravel and disintegrate, but another school of thought says that it has already sustained the worst and will survive. I don't know about you, but I would never want to bet against the survival of any government entitlement program. Legislators will always figure out a way to bail it out, or, if it is beyond all repair, they might just take the easy route and opt for a single-payer system, which was Obama's plan all along. That's the worst of all worlds.

Even if Obamacare's ultimate failure were inevitable, Republicans can't sit on their hands and watch it die in slow motion. Far too many people will be hurt, which is unacceptable.

Moreover, though many Republicans assume that Obamacare's final implosion would mostly redound to the Democrats' detriment, it is hard to see that considering they would be the ones in power during the implosion. Don't ever underestimate the formidability of the media-enabled Democratic propaganda machine.

If Republicans don't get their act together now, they may not ever get another chance to prevent socialized medicine in this country. We'll never have a better chance to make market-based health care reforms if we don't pass the best bill possible now, for at least two reasons: First, Republicans will be punished for incompetence and betrayal in the next election. And second, there will be a point beyond which market reforms can't feasibly be made.

But if Republicans move this bill through, there's a good chance they can continue to improve it incrementally — especially if the changes in the current bill yield demonstrable results.

The proposed Senate bill is far from perfect, but we're fantasizing if we think we're going to get anything close to perfect at this point. Sen. Ted Cruz apparently finds the bill acceptable, and, for now, all things considered, that's good enough for me.

Pseudo-Republican Squishes Are Anything but Compassionate

July 28, 2017

It is enormously frustrating that conservatives can't capture the moral high ground from the phony virtue-signaling factory that is the modern Democratic Party. Conservative policies not only work better but also are morally superior.

Democrats depend on cliches and false narratives to obstruct true reform — which includes shaming many Republicans from believing enough in their own agenda to pursue it with conviction. This is nowhere more apparent than in the endless debate over the fate of Obamacare and the future of American health care.

It is unconscionable that Republicans are unable to muster a simple majority to end the Obamacare monstrosity — a freakish beast that does everything it promised not to do and does little it promised to do, a gargantuan scam that is destroying our health care, eroding our liberty and punishing our economy. It's a camel with its entire body already inside the tent of the American idea — hellbent on completing Obama's plan to fundamentally demolish it.

It's almost a waste of space to reiterate the obvious truth that the Democratic Party is bankrupt. It is wholly out of ideas except for concocting ever more creative ways to demonize conservatives as bigots, thwart policies that could bring relief to the people it professes to champion, and advance an agenda whose inevitable result is socialism — all while pretending to believe in free market competition.

Democrats mouth such banalities as offering a "better deal," as if they weren't the ones who have given us this horrendous deal that is rotting the American system from the inside out.

They are incapable of offering new ideas because they are ideologically and politically enslaved. Their worldview weds them to the historically discredited notion that great results flow from allegedly good intentions. And their lust for power impels them to exploit identity politics and perpetuate victimhood for the constituencies whose overwhelming support is essential to their political lifeblood.

For example, they can't support decentralization and competition in education, no matter how much that could improve the lives of minorities trapped in inferior schools, or support across-the-board tax cuts — even though cuts for higher-income earners help stimulate economic growth, which redounds to the benefit of middle- and lower-income earners — because they cannot abandon their class warfare strategy.

Now back to today's more pressing issue — health care reform. Their policies have wrought untold disaster across the board, yet they will acknowledge no responsibility for these failures, much less join, in any way, those seeking solutions.

Democrats tell us they would be happy to work with Republicans to repair the glitches in Obamacare. The problem is that we are not dealing with mere glitches. The entire legislative debacle is a galloping cancer on our system.

Further exposing the Democrats' fraud, almost all of the Republicans' so-called "repeal and replace" proposals have not actually contemplated repeal at all; they've just proposed revisions. Yet Democrats, in lockstep, will not even come to the table to discuss them. In other words, except for their failed efforts to fully repeal the bill, all Republican proposals have been efforts not to completely end Obamacare (sad to say) but to partially repair it.

Democrats don't want the system improved. They know it's a barely disguised wealth redistribution scheme that if left alone will necessarily eventuate in a single-payer system — a euphemism for socialized medicine.

So for now, let's forget Democrats, who have no intention of working with Republicans on this.

What about the couple of handfuls of pseudo-Republicans who don't have the decency to end this nightmare — the ones who campaigned on the promise to repeal this law but won't now pull the trigger?

I don't want to hear that their consciences are involved or that they are from liberal states. How about their intellectual honesty and dignity?

Why do they enable Democratic propaganda that millions would be hurt by repealing a law that forces those millions to buy insurance against their will? Why aren't they held accountable for giving life-support to a law that is already harming people and would result in socializing one-sixth of our economy?

Don't you just love hearing the self-serving protestations of these squishes, pretending to care so much about people while they are single-handedly (as Democratic intransigence is an irremediable reality) decimating world history's greatest health care system?

There is nothing compassionate about what Democrats and their sanctimonious foxhole-sharing Republican frauds are doing here.

It's time for freedom-loving, people-loving Americans to turn the tables on these charlatans and recapture the moral high ground through aggressive and intelligent messaging. We'll never save this republic if we can't make the case that government largesse is fundamentally destructive and incompetent and that the invisible hand of the market yields results across the board that are more beneficial for more people than those of any other system known to man.

Socialism kills, impoverishes and enslaves and only masquerades as compassion while facilitating the compassion merchants' consolidation of power. Freedom brings prosperity and, if you insist on using compassion as the be-all-end-all yardstick, is abundantly compassionate.

Major Acosta Fail

August 4, 2017

On Wednesday, CNN's Jim Acosta unwittingly demonstrated the difference between an unbiased, truth-seeking media and a biased, hostile and advocacy media.

We need a watchdog press in this country, but its proper function is to report the news, not become the story. Acosta had displayed his obnoxiousness before, but he descended to a new low this week.

Earlier in the day, President Trump had appeared with Sens. Tom Cotton and David Perdue to endorse their immigration bill, called the RAISE Act. The bill was the major focus of the White House press briefing, and presidential adviser Stephen Miller outlined its key elements.

Miller's presentation was hijacked by Acosta, who is apparently on a crusade to establish himself as America's conscience and chief protector against President Trump.

We've all seen the give-and-take of White House news conferences, and they sometimes involve feisty exchanges between the administration's spokesperson and members of the media. But there is a difference between a journalist respectfully challenging the White House representative and a militant advocate posing as a journalist and disrespectfully interrupting, disrupting, speechifying and trying to make himself the star of the show.

Acosta put on a clinic on how not to behave in such settings and illustrated why ordinary Americans are so distrustful of the mainstream liberal media.

The proposed legislation would mark a significant overhaul of the nation's legal immigration policy. Currently, our system substantially burdens taxpayers and the economy. More than half of immigrant households receive welfare benefits, whereas only 30 percent of native households receive welfare. Existing policies discourage assimilation and hardly incentivize learning English.

Moreover, the system has attracted low-skilled and unskilled immigrants into the country. According to the White House, only 1 in 15 immigrants enter the nation because of their skills. The overwhelming majority of the 1 million immigrants who enter each year are low-skilled or unskilled.

The RAISE Act addresses these problems directly, by replacing the permanent employment-visa structure with a skills-based system. Applicants would be considered based on their education, ability to speak English, high-paying job offers, past achievements and entrepreneurial initiative. Canada and Australia use similar merit-based approaches.

While continuing to prioritize immediate family members of U.S. residents, the bill would end preferences for extended family members and adult children. It would also limit the number of refugees who get permanent resident status to 50,000 per year.

This is a serious proposal and one consistent with President Trump's campaign promises on immigration. It would benefit America and our culture and would reduce the welfare burden imposed under the current system.

Unsurprisingly, certain liberal and mainstream media members are none too pleased with the plan. Acosta made that quite clear, treating the White House press briefing more like an inquisition than a fact-finding opportunity.

Sneeringly, Acosta attacked Miller, painting the proposal as racist and discriminatory. He implied the policy would violate the welcoming spirit of the Statue of Liberty toward the tired and poor of other nations.

Acosta seemed outraged that the bill would require immigrants to speak English, saying it suggests the administration is trying to engineer the racial and ethnic flow of people into the country.

Miller did not accept this claim passively, countering that it was one of the most outrageous, ignorant, insulting and foolish things Acosta had ever said.

Acosta was particularly hostile and rude, making pointed statements masked as questions, refusing to allow Miller the courtesy of responding and repeatedly interrupting him. It was as if Acosta imagined himself on the CNN debate show "Crossfire," forgot to do his homework and assumed he would be declared the winner if he monopolized the exchange with rudeness, arrogance, volume and ignorance.

A less insolent human being, after having thus misbehaved, would be repentant and wish he could erase the horrific episode. Not so with Acosta, who, after reflecting, doubled down in a discussion with Wolf Blitzer, saying the "White House has an unhealthy fixation on what I call the three M's — the Mexicans, the Muslims and the media. Their policies tend to be crafted around bashing one of those three groups, and we just see it time and again."

As a self-righteous liberal, Acosta simply must impugn conservatives in the administration every time he gets a chance. So twisted is he that he apparently believes that those who support assimilation and a common language are bigots. Unless you promote open borders and Balkanization, you must hate people of different ethnicities.

Given such toxic biases, it's no wonder Americans rarely have good-faith, constructive debates on pressing issues. With such misguided finger-pointing, it's no wonder most people are appalled at the monolithic mainstream media.

I don't ordinarily use the term "fake news," but there was nothing remotely authentic about Acosta's disgraceful performance and even less that resembled an unbiased approach to the facts.

I sincerely hope that Acosta and his like-minded colleagues continue in this posture, further exposing themselves as the preening, demagogic leftist partisans they are.

It's 1984 at Google

August 11, 2017

Google's firing of software engineer James Damore for daring to express politically incorrect ideas in an internal memo is the latest example of the political left's tyrannical propensity to suppress speech, thought and dissent.

Almost as troubling as the left's policing is its apparent obliviousness toward its own hypocrisy and the danger it poses to the liberal exchange of ideas. While constitutional issues may not be involved in the Google case because no state action is involved, moral shaming has become a chilling cudgel in the hands of leftist-dominated institutions.

In his memo, Damore notes that Google's political bias silences dissenting opinion supposedly to shield employees from offensive ideas and protect their psychological safety. "But shaming into silence," writes Damore, "is the antithesis of psychological safety. This silencing has created an ideological echo chamber where some ideas are too sacred to be honestly discussed."

Damore concedes that all people have biases but that open and honest discussion can highlight these biases and help us grow. He says he wrote the memo to encourage such a discussion about Google's biases, a discussion that is being silenced by "the dominant ideology."

Damore opines that both the political left and right have moral biases. "Only facts and reason can shed light on these biases," he says, "but when it comes to diversity and inclusion, Google's left bias has created a politically correct monoculture that maintains its hold by shaming dissenters into silence. This silence removes any checks against encroaching extremist and authoritarian policies."

He then details how this bias affects Google's explanation for the gender gap in the tech world and leadership positions: Its leftist bias tells it that the gap is due to differential treatment (discrimination and injustices). It then applies authoritarian measures that actually discriminate against men to achieve equal representation. This is the wrong approach, says Damore, because the gender gap is partially attributable to many biological differences between men and women, and because there are "non-discriminatory ways to reduce the gender gap."

Stated more simply, biologically based differences between the sexes in certain abilities and preferences, as opposed to gender bias and discrimination, are why there are fewer women in tech jobs and leadership positions. Redistributing these positions could be more harmful than helpful to employees and the company. We should think of people as individuals, not as interchangeable members of groups.

It's ironic that such leftist thinking purports to enhance the worth of women (or members of other allegedly victimized groups) but instead disrespects and devalues their human dignity by imposing groupwide remedies without regard to individual qualities and behavior.

We must recognize that Damore is making two separate but interrelated complaints. He is saying that Google is applying totalitarian groupthink to its gender bias problem and thus misanalyzing it; and that this same groupthink also prevents open and honest discussion of the problem by forbidding the expression of dissenting views.

It's one thing for Google honchos to strongly disagree with the thrust of Damore's substantive arguments concerning the reasons for the gender gap. But it's quite another for them to effectively ban dissent and summarily fire him for dissenting.

But this is nothing new for the left. For example, many leftists seek to ban debate on "climate change" through cultural fiat, declaring that an irrefutable scientific consensus has been established. In the name of science — which by definition demands that such issues always remain open to challenge — they shut down dissent. Similarly, they say certain views will not be tolerated on college campuses because they are offensive to certain people. On many of these same campuses, they commit violence to people and property to protest conservative speakers whose speech they think could lead to violence. Such preposterous thinking is as widespread as it is ludicrous. Through sophistry and semantic legerdemain, the left has ushered in an era of intellectual anarchy.

Leftists see themselves as stewards of enlightened thinking — of liberal academic inquiry, tolerance and diversity — but once again, they prove themselves to be Stalinist tailors of intellectual straightjackets who flagrantly violate the very spirit of free expression on which America was founded.

Leftists are ingenious manufacturers of twisted excuses to justify their indefensible actions. But intellectual honesty screams for an accounting in these cases. They might be fooling themselves into believing they are advancing the greater good, but they're not fooling those outside the intellectual prisons of their pride-spawned, self-congratulatory oppression.

The Tragedy and Exploitation of Charlottesville

August 18, 2017

The inexhaustible left is perpetually lying in wait to entrap President Donald Trump in some impeachable offense. Sadly, some vocal Trump critics on the right seem just as eager to purge America of Trump.

They hate him and hate that he won, and their impeachment lust will not be satiated until he's gone.

The Trump haters on the right are one thing. But don't be deceived into believing that the anti-Trump angst factories on the left are only about Trump. To be sure, these leftists hate Trump with a white-hot passion, but their primary goal is to thwart, suppress and ultimately silence political conservatism. It is to reinvigorate Barack Obama's failed progressive agenda by any means necessary.

If Trump weren't president, the left's monomaniacal zeal to obliterate all things conservative would be unabated. Though Trump often makes their job easier, they would savage any Republican president, including the venerable Vice President Mike Pence, should he later ascend to the office. They'd maul Pence for his unapologetically Christian and social conservative views and paint him as an unmitigated bigot.

No matter what you think of the Charlottesville tragedy, in a limited but significant sense, it has become leftists' new Russia — for as long as they can get mileage out of it. It is liberals' latest best chance to discredit Trump and his agenda and run him out of town on a humiliating impeachment rail — and into the hoosegow to boot, if possible.

How ironic that these rule of law-defying opportunists are champing at the bit to impeach Trump in the name of the rule of law. They couldn't care less about whether he's committed any impeachable offenses under the Constitution. For them, his impeachability inheres in his political views. It predates his inauguration — and persists. Right-wingers, whether conservative ideologues or not, are intrinsically bigoted. Trump's alleged boorishness, his lack of filter and, most of all, his tweets are just icing on the cake. Leftists shouldn't have to tolerate occupancy of the Oval Office by a man so repugnant to them. So, the will of the people and the electoral process be damned, Trump must go. They will not rest until something they throw against the wall sticks.

With Collusiongate having failed them so far, they believe they've finally hit pay dirt with Charlottesville. When you cut through all the clutter and noise, it seems that Trump's main sin was saying that both sides were at fault and that there were good people on both sides of the protest.

If I thought that by this Trump meant that there are good people among neo-Nazis and white supremacists, I would join in the strong criticism. And I admit he could have been more artful. If you are predisposed to believe that Trump is a racist, you'll probably find something in his statement to support your predisposition.

But I don't believe for a second that Trump is a racist or that he approves of white supremacy, neo-Nazism, anti-Semitism or any other form of racism or bigotry. I think that what he meant was that there are good people among those defending the monuments. And it appears that most Americans agree with that, despite the media's conscious effort to suggest otherwise. Recent polls show that some 62 percent of Americans support preserving the monuments as historic symbols, and 67 percent of Republicans approve of Trump's statement on Charlottesville. Do any of you really want to claim that 62 percent of Americans or 67 percent of Republicans are bigots?

I don't think I'm exaggerating when I say many leftists do indeed believe that. Indeed, isn't that really at the heart of this flap? Aren't Trump's critics implying, in the end, that he's a racist — or at the very least that his statement was a dog whistle to white supremacists because he believes they are an important part of his base? Are they implying that those who continue to support him are also stained by bigotry?

I don't believe that more than the slightest fraction of a percentage of Trump supporters are neo-Nazis or white supremacists just because some of these Neanderthals choose to praise or champion Trump. I further reject that neo-Nazis, fascists and white supremacists are politically conservative, but the left's historical revisionism enables it to smear the entire right wing with this bilious claim.

Some leftists have suggested that Trump was trying to create moral equivalence between the extremists on the left and the neo-Nazis, indignantly describing the leftist protesters as innocuous, noble opponents of slavery and bigotry who have no other agenda than to register their dissent against these white supremacists.

Please don't accuse me of deflecting or defending the abhorrent white supremacists for this, but I am not going to sit idly by while this kind of wretched propaganda is disseminated. These misnamed leftist antifa are anti-fascist in name only and are anything but innocent. They are community organizers, often bused in from afar and funded by leftist Alinskyites to create havoc, chaos and political, social and racial unrest throughout the nation. They are up to no good, and though I won't fall into the trap of attempting to compare the relative evils of these various groups and thereby be painted as being soft on racism, I will not be intimidated into silence about them.

Wouldn't it be glorious if the media devoted just one-third of the time they spend trashing Trump to covering his policy agenda — albeit as unfair as that reportage would be? America is still stinging from the Obama years and before, and we all need to focus less on hate and angst and more on true reforms that could benefit the American people.

The violence and murder in Charlottesville are indefensible, abhorrent and gut-wrenching, and I pray that we can cut through shameless efforts at political exploitation and learn constructive lessons from this.

Trump Movement Transcends Trump
August 25, 2017

Do you equal-opportunity Trump haters ever listen to yourselves? You sometimes remind me of the people in those movies who live the same day over and over.

You must wake up every day — wholly oblivious to your behavior the day before — gleefully imagining how you could dismantle Trump with a single tweet, a doleful column or a brief television critique. Even if your criticisms sound new to you, most of us were here yesterday — and during the days, weeks and months leading up to yesterday. What you are offering is not profound.

Sometimes the absurdity reaches comical proportions. You figuratively subject Trump to rapid machine-gun fire every day and then lay your weapons down, walk over to the camera and castigate Trump for bleeding.

Yes, some of Trump's abrasions are self-inflicted, but anyone under ceaseless fire like him would be hard-pressed not to overreact from time to time.

The news media — almost all on the left and too many on the right — make every news cycle about Trump. It's not about North Korea's nuclear weapons, Afghanistan, immigration, health care or radical Islam. It's about Trump. Every story is centered on him.

And don't tell me this is only because Trump makes everything about himself. Oh, yes, he personalizes things, but we're not talking about him; we're talking about you. You make it about him — and about yourselves and your moral superiority for condemning him as a Neanderthal every five minutes.

We get it. Republican Trump supporters disgrace themselves. After all, according to many of you, Trump would have no support among conservative commentators and media figures if they listened to their consciences. No, they've all sold out.

Apparently, I can't be a constitutional conservative and support Trump, so I must be doing it for ratings on a show I don't have or Twitter likes, though I've yet to figure out how to monetize my betrayal.

But enough about me. How about people who do have shows and make their living through commentary? Well, I know a lot of them personally, and I don't know any who support Trump because they think it will enhance their ratings. It's not that they don't try to get ratings. But they don't support Trump as a means to that end.

Go ahead and laugh. But your automatic assumption that such conservative support for Trump must be political prostitution possibly reflects a hint of narrow arrogance. Trump is so manifestly egregious there could be no logical reason a bona fide conservative could support him. Right?

Let me respectfully suggest that Trump hasn't changed in office. He is the same person we saw on the campaign trail and the same person the American people elected as their 45th president. He was every bit as brash, unfiltered and unorthodox as he is now, so the next time you rush to your computer or microphone to declare his instability or unfitness for office, remember that the American people knowingly elected him as just that guy. Therefore, when you are impugning him, you might as well be (and often are) impugning them.

Now let me further shock you. They didn't elect Trump because they thought he was some panacea or some perfect cult hero. Yes, there are some Trump supporters who appear to be cultlike in their support, but I dare say that even most of them view Trump less as someone who is perfect and more as one who is in the foxhole with them trying to fight the forces determined to dismantle America as founded, piece by piece.

I acknowledge Trump's uniqueness and that he may have been the only one who could have satisfied the grass roots in 2016. But I think the Trump movement transcends Trump. It preceded him but coalesced in him and will survive him. You won't eradicate the

Trump movement by removing Trump — assuming that's your endgame.

You complain that Trump's peculiar mix of policy hodgepodge under the Republican banner is destroying the conservative and Republican brands. I used to be more sympathetic to that argument. But the problem is that Republicans have not been able (and often haven't seemed willing) to fight back against this leftist juggernaut that represents an existential threat to all we hold sacred. So many of them would haughtily scoff at the mere suggestion that we face existential threats in that context.

Conceding that Trump is no conservative ideologue by any stretch and still clinging to my self-identification as a Reagan and Ted Cruz conservative, I think we have a far better chance of thwarting the leftist agenda and recapturing lost territory under someone like Trump — as opposed to some well-mannered, leftist-appeasing centrist — who is willing and determined to fight.

You can be sure that the calculating left will be just as militant no matter who is in power. In fact, if members of some sordid bipartisan coalition are able to claim Trump's political scalp based on the stuff they're now throwing against the wall against him, there's no telling how emboldened the left will become. If you can live with that, it might be time for you to quit moralizing to us.

You might be deluding yourself if you think Trump will implode. You can read the polls and think he's finished or conclude that the latest tweetstorm is the final nail. But you will be wrong.

Some of you should quit worrying so much about conflating ideologies. The rise of so-called populist nationalism would have far less traction if the right showed much greater solidarity in standing up for the American idea, which is not about ethnicity, race, gender or diversity but about liberty, equal opportunity, a strong and unashamed America, and the rule of law. Advocating all these noble principles in theory alone will no longer be sufficient. We must get in the fight.

I love pure constitutional conservatism, perhaps as much as anyone, but way too many people who don't love it are pretending they do and using Trump as a scapegoat to cover for their failure to fight for the principles and policies they profess to champion.

I'm not suggesting that you shouldn't legitimately criticize Trump when he deserves it or that you abandon your principles. But please take your blinders off and get off your high horse.

If those of you who can't quit salivating over your next Trump dump would spend just a fourth of that time registering outrage over the stuff regularly spewing from the left — including the mainstream media — maybe you would do your part in helping to close the void that was filled by Donald Trump. Until our side recognizes the gravity of our situation and unifies to fight against the left with the same commitment the left brings to this fight, you can be sure that at least a strong plurality of the political right will continue to rally around unorthodox figures who at least have the brass to fight back.

President Trump Must Take Charge on Tax Reform

September 1, 2017

If you thought the left weaponized class warfare rhetoric in the health care debate, just wait until tax reform is front and center. The fate of this reform will depend on President Trump's leadership and GOP conviction.

The importance of Republican conviction goes without saying, right? Perhaps, but that doesn't mean we need to just accept GOP fecklessness and incompetence and quit talking about it. Eventually, President Trump's success and future GOP congressional majorities depend on whether Republicans really stand for their core values and the positions nominally affirmed in their platform. Reducing the tax burden on corporations and businesses is on any conservative's shortlist.

Republicans need to think through this and decide what their goals are. Are they really about maximizing liberty, reducing government (taxes and regulations) and stimulating economic growth — and not just paying lip service?

The positive business atmosphere Trump's victory ushered in and his market-friendly attitude have already yielded significantly positive results. We've just seen quarterly growth reach 3 percent. The stock market is thriving. Unemployment is down. Manufacturing is up. Overall, businesses are poised for growth.

Trump has done more than just champion business through his bully pulpit. He's reduced onerous regulations, taken steps to loosen the left's environmental straitjacket and issued orders to revive the

Keystone XL and Dakota Access pipeline projects as part of a comprehensive rejection of Obama's war on conventional energy.

But these advancements and numerous others will represent a hollow victory if pro-growth tax reform legislation isn't passed in the near future.

Given guaranteed Democratic demagoguery and mainstream-media propaganda, President Trump and his rudderless Republican congressional majorities have their work cut out for them.

I believe that President Trump made a mistake in his handling of health care reform by not commandeering the leadership role. It wasn't enough for him to say he would sign whatever bill the Republicans passed. He needed to embrace and articulate concrete and detailed policy objectives. For whatever reason, he didn't clearly and forcefully present his policy goals, much less propose specific provisions to effectuate them. He can't make that mistake with tax reform.

It's true that bills originate and must be passed in Congress before they get to the president, but effective reforming presidents have historically led or co-led major pieces of legislation for which they have later been credited.

Just look at how instrumental President Obama was in passing Obamacare. Likewise, on major tax reform legislation, who can deny President John F. Kennedy's pivotal role in passing marginal income tax cuts?

To be sure, Rep. Jack Kemp helped inspire the Reagan tax cuts, but President Reagan personally invested himself and his legacy in passage of his first major tax bill, which reduced marginal income tax rates by 25 percent across the board.

Reagan went over the heads of the liberal media and took his case to the American people. He had been a fierce advocate for personal liberty and the free market long before he took office, so he was particularly equipped to argue his case to the American jury.

Reagan didn't approach the issue one-dimensionally. Yes, he explained that individual and corporate earnings were first the property of individuals and corporations and not the government — rejecting the liberal notion that all property is the government's and the people are entitled to only what the leviathan, in its beneficence, allows them to retain. He also pleaded the tougher case that reductions in marginal rates spur economic growth by providing economic incentives and unleashing the power of the market.

President Reagan, certain congressional leaders and other thought leaders were intellectually grounded in every aspect of these issues and, just as importantly, truly believed in what they were selling. One of the most inspiring political books I've ever read was "An American Renaissance," by Jack Kemp, who eloquently laid out the rudimentary concept that a rising tide lifts all boats. Contrary to the then-universally accepted Keynesian notion, Kemp argued we could enjoy economic growth without inflation. The late William F. Buckley was a great admirer of Kemp's in those days and marveled at his contagious enthusiasm in presenting his ideas. Too bad we couldn't bottle that up and use it now.

History vindicated Reagan and Kemp. We experienced unprecedented economic growth without inflation, and the plight of all income groups, from the lowest 20 percent of earners to the highest 20 percent, improved. President Clinton's revisionism notwithstanding, the Reagan tax record is powerful and irrefutable. I am not denying that monetary policy was important, as well, but the tax cuts were paramount.

I would respectfully urge President Trump to approach tax reform wholly differently than he did with health care reform. I'd love it if he would read Kemp's book, become a true believer — even more than he is now — and take the lead role in shaping and driving this legislation through Congress. If he doesn't stake out a firm policy position, he will have no credibility or leverage to push congressional foot-draggers.

It won't do for Trump to telegraph his flexibility — telling GOP lawmakers he'll sign whatever they send him. He needs to be engaged and first send them a bold blueprint that evidences his confidence in the drive, ingenuity and sheer economic power of the American individual when unshackled from the chains of the federal government. He must not succumb to pressure to punish the so-called wealthy unless he wants to sabotage his own efforts.

We must remember that some 50 percent of Americans don't even pay income taxes, which is astonishing on multiple levels. The so-called wealthy already pay more than their fair share, so let's not go wobbly trying to defend lies to the contrary. Enough will never be enough for the demagogic left.

President Trump must be prepared to make the case that for tax cuts to work as intended — to actually stimulate growth — they must be across-the-board and substantial. This is the time for him to make a defining statement on economic policy and to take charge. My copy of "An American Renaissance" is available.

Sens. Feinstein and Durbin
Are Fooling No One

September 8, 2017

It's rich that rule of law-scoffing Democratic Sens. Dianne Feinstein and Dick Durbin grilled one of President Trump's judicial nominees, law professor Amy Coney Barrett, for placing her religious beliefs above the law.

During Barrett's appearance before the Senate Judiciary Committee on Wednesday, Durbin asked her, "Do you consider yourself an orthodox Catholic?"

Apparently, Durbin thought he had Barrett dead to rights because of assertions she made in a law review article she co-wrote with her law professor in 1998 as a third-year student at Notre Dame Law School. In the article, "Catholic Judges in Capital Cases," the authors discussed the question of whether "orthodox" Catholic judges (and other judges morally opposed to the death penalty) should sit in death penalty cases.

In these cases, the judges are faced with the dilemma of being bound "by oath, professional commitment, and the demands of citizenship to enforce the death penalty" while "also (being) obliged to adhere to their church's teaching on moral matters."

On reviewing the Roman Catholic Church's teachings and the relevant federal statutes, the authors concluded that judges faced with such a dilemma should recuse themselves in applicable cases, thereby honoring their moral duty without violating their legal duty.

In an explanatory footnote, the authors explained they were using the term "orthodoxy" in a limited context to describe those following the church's teachings on this issue. They were careful to note that they weren't casting aspersions on the overall faith of Catholics who don't adhere to the church's teachings on the death penalty.

Seizing on the term, Durbin thought he would corner Barrett into admitting that she is an "orthodox" Catholic, presumably to impugn her as some Roman Catholic fundamentalist whose religious extremism would lead her to flout the Constitution. Durbin's slimy distortion of Barrett's unambiguous words revealed that he either hadn't read her article or deliberately twisted her meaning. In this sleazy effort to entrap Barrett in a constitutional snare, Durbin landed himself in one of his own, because it is inappropriate for a senator to ask such a question of a judicial nominee, as the Constitution prohibits religious tests of any public officer.

Sen. Feinstein's questioning was just as odious, as she upbraided Barrett for her Catholic faith, saying, "The dogma lives loudly within you, and that's of concern."

It's particularly reprehensible for these secular-virtue-signaling senators to invoke their pernicious little trick bag to discredit Barrett because in her law review article, she explicitly addressed this very question and left no doubt that the law must control.

Indeed, the entire point of the article was to acknowledge and seek resolution for a judge's dilemma in this very situation. Shamefully, the scolding senatorial duo intentionally ignored Barrett's emphatic assertion that "judges cannot — nor should they try to — align our legal system with the Church's moral teaching whenever the two diverge."

That is, Barrett unequivocally affirmed judges' duty to the Constitution and the law and concluded that a judge may not superimpose her religious beliefs onto the legal system. The senators ignored that because it dispositively negates the impression they wanted to create with their questioning — that Barrett would subordinate the law to her religious beliefs.

Isn't it comical that these two senators were feigning fealty to the rule of law when the Democratic Party advocates an activist judiciary, whereby judges make laws instead of merely interpreting them?

The senators are not concerned about the integrity of the law. They are just hostile to those with a decidedly Christian worldview, even if in this particular case the Catholic position happens to generally align with the politically liberal view on the death penalty.

Sadly, the modern liberal position concerning so-called church-and-state issues has become increasingly extreme. Liberals are no longer satisfied with their already bloated interpretation of the First Amendment's establishment clause, which was originally designed to prevent the federal government from establishing a national church or religion. They've long been trying to remove most symbols and expressions of Christianity from the public square — even sometimes when the connection with the federal, state, county or local government is merely tenuous.

But now they are going even further, suggesting that the personal religious beliefs of public officials in any branch or level of government — not just the judiciary — should in no way influence their policy preferences. The absurdity of this should be obvious to any fair and reasonable observer. The policy preferences of every human being — and thus every public officeholder — are necessarily informed by his or her worldview.

Let's just ask the senators whether their own worldview leads them to oppose the death penalty and, if so, whether that worldview would prevent them from following the law in death penalty cases. Better yet, would their worldview — religious or not — lead them to ignore and rewrite the law in any other areas, such as abortion, immigration, health care and taxes?

We know the answer. Ends-justify-the-means leftists, almost to a man (or woman), have no hesitation in subordinating the law to their policy goals. It's only when a Republican officeholder or nominee is openly Christian that they get worked up about this. But as usual, their simulated concern is misplaced, because Christian constitutionalists are the last people they need to fear in such cases. As adherents to the rule of law, they will not, no matter how religious (or "orthodox") they are, ignore the law.

Despite their posturing, Durbin and Feinstein know that most liberal senators wouldn't even face a dilemma in such cases. If the existing law doesn't suit them and they don't have the political clout to amend it through the proper legislative process, they'll just ignore it as a bygone relic. They are fooling no one.

Holding Trump Accountable When Necessary

September 15, 2017

What is Donald Trump up to, and what are his supporters to do? Is Trump betraying his supporters, or are Chuck, Nancy and the media misrepresenting his position?

For the hundredth time, I supported Ted Cruz, not Trump, for the GOP presidential nomination. But when Trump was victorious, I supported him against Hillary Clinton, and I have no regrets about that because though Trump sometimes disappoints, Clinton would have been a wholesale nightmare. Even in hindsight, it's not a close call.

I have also criticized a small fraction of conservative pundits for their seemingly obsessive knee-jerk opposition to Trump and their apparent glee when he sometimes lives down to their expectations. My main objection to some never-Trumpers is their gratuitous piling on and apparent joy in doing so, even on unfair allegations, such as those of pre-election collusion with Russia. None of us should be motivated by bragging rights — the dubious satisfaction of saying "I told you so," especially when the interests of the nation hang in the balance.

Since the primaries, I have hoped that despite my doubts about Trump's allegiance to certain conservative principles, he would be able to advance a conservative agenda more than a centrist Republican could or would. This is not because he is a so-called outsider but mainly because he has shown a willingness to fight. Whatever else you might say about the Republican Party, it has lost its backbone, particularly on budget battles.

But the courage to fight is meaningless unless you are willing to fight for the right things. Given Trump's general non-ideological bent, why should his feistiness give us any solace?

Good question.

Well, Trump campaigned mostly as a conservative, and if the campaign showed him anything, it is that leftists — no matter what he may have learned living his entire life in liberal New York City — are his sworn enemies. If he hadn't chosen sides before, he had no choice now. If he hadn't been paying much attention to ideological issues before, he surely was learning now and becoming more conservative in the process.

No, I had no illusions that Trump had converted overnight to constitutional conservatism, but I was hopeful that he would make significant strides in rolling back Barack Obama's agenda. I sincerely want to hold on to that optimism.

Recently, however, Trump has given many of his supporters pause — including even some of the die-hardiest of the die-hards. Others in his camp are impervious to any evidence that Trump is faltering or is capable of it. Still others define what is good by whatever Trump does, just as some define what is bad by whatever he does, and those types are unreachable anyway.

A debate has emerged among certain Trump supporters over whether he has betrayed them by cozying up to Democratic leaders or he is playing some elaborate version of 4-D chess. Those unfazed by Trump's two-step with Pelosi and Schumer are ecstatic that he is finally taking it to Ryan and McConnell. But it will be a cold day in Hades before I rejoice in Trump's humiliating establishment Republicans when it comes at the price of abandoning his campaign pledges and a mainstream conservative agenda. Let's not lose our heads.

Admittedly, political analysis is difficult in such a chaotic, convoluted, paradigm-shifting environment. The stakes are enormously high. There are many moving parts. Political constituencies are more fluid than they've been in decades. And there is an unusually high level of intramural tension in the Republican Party. Arguably, even the conservative movement is experiencing an identity crisis, with chest thumpers from all sides claiming they are the true conservatives and everyone else is a fraud.

For me, the jury is still out. Yes, Trump is making me nervous sometimes. Reports of his vacillation wouldn't bother me so much except for his history of sympathy for certain liberal issues, his basic non-ideological bent, his desire for personal approval, his focus on the deal-making process (as distinguished from the goals to be achieved in the deals) and the presence in his inner circle of socially liberal influencers. How, then, can we not be uneasy when we read that Trump's tax cuts will punish the "wealthy," that he's abandoning his opposition to amnesty or his commitment to the wall and that he's losing interest in undoing the Iranian nuclear deal?

You feel me?

I don't want to rush to judgment and prefer to believe that Trump will quit going wobbly and make course adjustments back toward those who brought him to the dance. For the record, I happen to believe that those who brought him to the dance are essentially conservatives — not populists, racists or political cultists.

I never want to pile on Trump with those malevolently motivated to destroy him. But his opponents' bad faith must not blind us to his missteps or silence us about his policy betrayals, should they occur. Political leaders must be held accountable, sometimes on a daily basis. This is for their own good, as well as the nation's.

Just this week, we read reports of Trump's alleged deals with Democrats, and within a few hours, after significant blowback from Trump supporters, he raced to Twitter and public microphones to assure us he isn't fishtailing on the wall.

At this point, it's difficult to tell whether the media reports were completely fallacious about Trump's caving or he actually did an immediate 180. Either way, we got strong and expeditious clarification — and that can only be healthy.

If Trump's supporters don't ever criticize him for fear of strengthening the position of his opponents, then he might just strengthen the position of his opponents on his own initiative. Trump is an old hand at business, but he is new at the game of politics, and the more constructive feedback he gets the better his governance will be.

Traditional Values Are White Supremacy?

September 22, 2017

Does the political left — which dominates the mainstream media, Hollywood, academia and the Democratic Party — really believe its ubiquitous charges of racism against conservatives, or are they a sick ploy to discredit, ruin and defeat its political opponents?

During President Obama's tenure, a conservative could hardly oppose Obama on policy grounds without being accused of racism. It didn't matter that conservatives had fought Hillary Clinton's health care plan in the '90s because they opposed socialized medicine. It didn't matter that they had opposed Bill Clinton's tax hikes. Their opposition to Obamacare and Obama's proposed tax increases had to be motivated by race.

If you repeat an absurd claim often enough, it becomes believable to some people. And the left has been hammering away so long against the supposed racism of political conservatives that many people, hordes of whom know better and multitudes of millennial political neophytes who apparently don't, have bought into this toxicity.

I have always assumed that one of the main reasons racism is sinful is that it involves judging people and discriminating against them not on the basis of their individual character or behavior but on their group identity. Among other things, this robs people of their human dignity and equal worth as being created in God's image.

It is noteworthy that the left — in its categorical condemnation of conservatives as racists — engages in the very type of discriminatory judgment it decries, i.e., says conservatives are racist because the policies they support allegedly hurt minorities.

But conservatives reject that their policies hurt minorities. We think history has shown that they help all people and that liberal policies are consistently destructive. Moreover, our policies, by definition, aspire to colorblindness. We believe in equality of opportunity for all and oppose policies tailored to race in application or result.

Conversely, policies driven by identity politics perpetuate tensions among different races. The damage done to race relations by an entire political wing bearing false witness against the other on race is incalculable. Can you imagine, for example, the harm that would befall my children and others if I poisoned them daily with the lie that certain people hate them?

It would be easier to understand this insanity if it could be explained simply by the left's cynical desire to exploit race for political gain. After all, liberals' constant agitation of minorities, with their 24/7 crusade against conservatives as racist, has to be primarily responsible for blacks' disproportionate support for the Democratic Party when the latter's policies have demonstrably harmed the plight of blacks.

But there seems to be something even more disturbing at play in this nonstop leftist slander. Look at the kind of poison emanating from universities throughout the United States.

Witness the recent brouhaha over a jointly penned op-ed by two law professors (Amy Wax of the University of Pennsylvania and Larry Alexander of the University of San Diego) who suggested, essentially, that America's decline can be traced to a rejection of traditional values (or, in the authors' words, "the breakdown of the country's bourgeois culture") and advocated a return to those values.

The professors argued that America did better when we had traditional values and therefore should return to this "cultural script": "Get married before you have children and strive to stay married for their sake. Get the education you need for gainful employment, work hard, and avoid idleness. Go the extra mile for your employer or client. Be a patriot, ready to serve the country. Be neighborly, civic-minded, and charitable. Avoid coarse language in public. Be respectful of authority. Eschew substance abuse and crime."

Significantly, the authors were careful to note that these "basic cultural precepts ... could be followed by people of all backgrounds and abilities." That is, the benefits of these values and practices transcend race.

Precisely on cue, however, leftist robot — aka University of Pennsylvania Law School dean — Ted Ruger charged to the student newspaper with an op-ed denouncing Wax's piece as divisive and noxious and rejecting "emphatically ... that a single cultural tradition is better than all others." Charges subsequently poured in from faculty members, students and alumni accusing Wax of white supremacy, misogyny and homophobia. Some demanded that she be barred from teaching first-year law courses.

Alexander experienced a similar backlash when University of San Diego School of Law Dean Stephen Ferruolo disseminated a schoolwide memo denouncing the piece, as well.

Regrettably, the left, in academia and elsewhere, increasingly equates traditional values (and political conservatism) with white supremacy. The norms that were formerly accepted almost universally are not just under systematic assault but also being indicted as racist.

Let me ask you sincerely: Do people really believe that these innocuous notions of hard work, virtue, marriage, respect, friendship, civic-mindedness, charity and patriotism are unique to certain races or groups of people? That they are not constructive goals for individuals, groups and the nation? That they are somehow rooted in bigotry of any kind?

The answer has to be "yes." Some really believe this nonsense, which means the left's propagation of these ideas is more than just a calculated ploy for power. And that's probably more alarming, because it means it is more deep-seated.

These corrosive ideas must be fought in the most aggressive terms. We simply won't be able to return this nation and its people to greatness, much less make strides in racial harmony, if we can't even try to improve ourselves without being accused of racism.

If we think we can ignore these cockeyed ideas as fringe and insignificant, then we are in denial. They are everywhere; they're no longer the stuff of radical anecdotes.

We'd better wake up — and stand up for the things we believe in, lest their very advocacy convict us soon of hate crimes warranting societal censure. At the risk of being falsely accused of white supremacy, may I suggest that we all become more civic-minded and charitable and promote the time-tested traditions that have made this nation great and that are designed to improve the lot of all people, irrespective of race, creed, ethnicity or gender?

Unfair Charges of Systemic Racism

September 29, 2017

No matter how often leftists slander conservatives as racists, no matter how much they try to shame NFL fans for objecting to players kneeling during the national anthem, flag-waving patriots are not going to be cowed into surrendering on this issue.

Why is it that anytime leftists engage in political debate or protest, no matter how inflammatory their content or manner of expression, they are glorified and defended? Conversely, why are conservatives automatically condemned as insensitive or censorious when they express their views or object to those of the left?

In this upside-down culture, the left is always treated as occupying the moral high ground, and criticism of liberals is deemed injurious to their right to free speech.

So when certain NFL players kneel during the national anthem, the dominant liberal media culture celebrates them, while anyone who objects to their action is accused of infringing on their liberties, even though no state action is involved and no constitutional question is at issue.

It is leftists who want to chill the speech of those criticizing the protesters for disrespecting the American flag. Instead of invoking bogus free speech issues, shouldn't we talk about the content of the protesters' complaints and the propriety of their manner of expressing them?

It seems the thrust of the protesters' complaint is that American law enforcement and America itself are systemically racist.

But if a protest movement seeks to be constructive, its complaints must be considered on the merits, and that means a full and substantive discussion of the facts. Those who disagree with the gravamen of the complaint have just as much right to express their opinion as the complainants. Bullying them into silence is hardly going to facilitate a resolution.

If the complainants truly are asserting that America's law enforcement institutions or America itself is systemically racist against African-Americans, they bear the burden of proving their assertions, especially when facts and statistics appear to contradict those claims. The Washington Post reports that of the 963 people shot and killed by police in America last year, only 17 of the victims were unarmed African-Americans. On its face, that's a troubling number, but it does not suggest systemic racism of law enforcement. This is not a dispositive statistic, but it is one that must be considered among others.

Lest you accuse me of exaggerating the protesters' position, note that I'm just listening to what many of them and their supporters say on national television and radio. Universities are replete with courses railing against white supremacy and racism in this country. The professional leftist protest cabal, antifa, is certainly making these claims unambiguously, and mainstream Democrats and the media are championing their cause. Antifa is so extreme on white privilege that you can sometimes hear its members berating fellow white colleagues for joining protests because they are "inherently racist."

No reasonable person can defend specific acts of racist behavior, especially by law enforcement officers. But protesters shouldn't get away with misstating facts to prove their claim. Such distortions cannot possibly help correct actual instances of racism. Protesters should be challenged, for example, if they claim racism is involved when a black officer shoots a black civilian. When protesters cite Michael Brown and Ferguson as an example of "hands up, don't shoot," they should be called out for misrepresenting the facts. Brown was not shot in the back by a police officer while peacefully trying to surrender, yet many have intentionally perpetuated that destructive myth.

People are tired of police officers being attacked and accused of systemic racism. The overwhelming majority of citizens would be appalled and outraged if they believed it were true. People are alarmed at being presumed racist based on the color of *their* skin. No one wants to be unjustly accused of racism — one of the most damning charges that could be leveled in our society. As the charge is so damaging, it shouldn't be made freely and indiscriminately or without a strong factual basis. Those who do systemically engage in such baseless accusations should themselves be condemned for it.

People are certainly free to claim America or American law enforcement is systemically racist, but fairness requires that they back up their claims factually.

Protesters are free to kneel during the national anthem, assuming the NFL chooses not to discipline them for rule violation, but fans are also free to express their disapproval of the protesters' overt disrespecting of the American flag.

Many fans believe that regardless of the merits of the protesters' claims, it is inappropriate for them to express their complaint in this form — because it implies, if not outright expresses, that the nation itself is somehow guilty of the type of racist behavior they are protesting.

Many Americans are fed up with the ongoing effort in our culture to trash this nation and its historical symbols — not just controversial Confederate symbols but many others, as well.

Evidence of racial tension in America is not limited to football players kneeling. There has been an ongoing effort by race agitators on the left to stir the pot for political and other reasons. A conservative can hardly take a political position on any issue, no matter how innocuous, without someone on the left's accusing him of racism. Talk about chilling speech and political dissent!

President Trump provides a convenient scapegoat for the left and many on the right. Criticize him if you must for fanning the flames, but don't fool yourself that he is responsible for the overall problem we face, which is serious and must be taken seriously. And be aware that many appreciate it when people in leadership positions defend the sanctity of the flag.

It should go without saying that racism of all kinds and in all directions is unacceptable, including unwarranted claims of racism, which are themselves grounded in race.

If protesters genuinely want their problems addressed, they must quit stating more than the facts allow, refrain from outrageous and damaging hyperbole, and support their specific claims with concrete evidence. And unless they want to continue to draw as much ire as they draw constructive attention to their concerns, they must quit targeting the American flag and other sacred national symbols.

The Left Just Isn't Right

October 13, 2017

Please join me on a whirlwind superficial but revealing tour of liberal la-la land as we peek at recent headlines. Meanwhile, liberals call conservatives wing nuts.

Singer Nancy Sinatra tweeted, "The murderous members of the NRA should face a firing squad." One wonders whether in her rendering, "murderous" is redundant. One might also wonder whether she thinks other murderous people should be exempt from or perhaps face a less humiliating form of execution.

Responding to Michelle Obama's claim that people are distrustful of politics because the GOP is "all men, all white," Rep. Mia Love, R-Utah, said, "I don't know if she noticed, but I am not white and I am not a male." To clarify, in case you are wondering, in this example, Michelle Obama is the inhabitant of la-la land.

Republican Rep. Marsha Blackburn of Tennessee, who is running for the Senate seat currently held by Bob Corker, encountered Twitter's speech police when trying to place an ad saying, "I fought Planned Parenthood, and we stopped the sale of baby body parts." Twitter's thought cops said the claim was "deemed an inflammatory statement that is likely to evoke a strong negative reaction." They magnanimously assured her that they'd run the ad if she removed the offending statement. If Twitter brass were truly concerned about tweets evoking "a strong negative reaction," the executives would save themselves time and just shut the whole operation down. If you use Twitter much, you know that evoking such reactions is virtually guaranteed in cultural and political tweets, which populate Twitter by the millions every day. It would be much easier to interact with leftists if they could at least be honest with themselves and others about what they are doing in these situations. They have no problem with tweets evoking strong negative reactions from conservatives. But you knew that.

ESPN anchor Jemele Hill last month faced no consequences for calling President Trump a white supremacist but was suspended for two weeks when she urged fans to boycott NFL advertisers because Dallas Cowboys owner Jerry Jones had threatened to bench players who refuse to stand during the national anthem. "Change happens when advertisers are impacted," she tweeted. "If you strongly reject what Jerry Jones said, the key is his advertisers. Don't place the burden squarely on the players." Twitter moguls apparently didn't deem Hill's tweets as likely to evoke a strong negative reaction. I wonder whether Hill would agree that her employer's reaction was neither strong nor negative. One person who doubtlessly wouldn't regard Hill's tweet as negative is ESPN's Michael Wilbon, who compared Jones to a slave owner because of his action.

The Daily Wire reported that activists of Abolish Human Abortion were booted from Bedlam Coffee in Seattle because the gay owner couldn't tolerate their presence. After asking members of the group whether they would tolerate his bringing his boyfriend in the shop and performing sex acts with him in front of them, he told them, "Well, then I don't have to f—-ing tolerate this! Then leave — all of you! Tell all your f—-ing friends, 'Don't f—-ing come here'!" I have no real problem with owners serving whom they choose in a free market, but I'll note that it's unlikely that we'll hear outcries from the left complaining about this discriminatory treatment because here those being denied service were not asking for a wedding cake for a same-sex marriage ceremony.

In case you haven't heard of the concept of "cultural appropriation," it is the use of certain aspects of a certain culture by another culture, which, to those who use the term, is a bad thing. Who thinks this way? But I digress. University of Texas cultural studies professor Luis Urrieta has taken the concept to a new level. Urrieta noted that these appropriations have "many economic, social and symbolic repercussions. The first is obviously the theft of intellectual property, the theft of communal knowledge. ... Socially, it reduces native and indigenous peoples to 'artifacts' that can be worn, used, consumed and displayed." A few examples of what they mean by "appropriation" will suffice to illustrate. The University of California, Merced told fraternities and sororities they should avoid using the terms "Greek," "rush" and "pledge" because they are appropriations of Greek culture. And at San Francisco State University, an African-American student reportedly attacked a white student because his hair was in dreadlocks. No, you really can't make this stuff up. "Appropriation is a form of theft," said Urrieta. "It is a nice way of saying that someone is taking someone else's (idea) and making it their own." In my humble view, the burden of defending such Twilight Zonery is on any who would defend it, but maybe I'm just old-fashioned. In case you think Urrieta is merely an outlier, another professor, Rachel V. Gonzalez-Martin, described cultural appropriation as "cultural poaching." If you're still thinking "outliers," the University of Michigan advertised to recruit a person — at an annual salary of $50,000 — to handle "cultural appropriation prevention activities." Don't laugh; this isn't satire.

Finally, California Gov. Jerry Brown recently signed legislation lowering from a felony to a misdemeanor the act of knowingly exposing a sexual partner to HIV without disclosing the infection to the person. Also protected by this outrageously reckless nod to political correctness are those who give blood without revealing their infection. Here I can't say "there are no words," because there are plenty, but I've run out of space.

For the same reason, I must omit tons of other examples, but in mitigation for this inadequacy, I think it is only fair that I get props for not opining on the Harvey Weinstein scandal, trusting that the news saturation on this story has reached your homes.

Media Ignore Real Democratic Scandals

October 20, 2017

Why the collective liberal media yawn on the multi-headed Democratic scandals surfacing everywhere except on their pages and airwaves?

It's not that the stories are too far-fetched and thin to interest self-respecting journalists, because they are real, damning and supported by sufficiently credible evidence to warrant serious attention and scrutiny.

There are the notorious Trump dossier, the Clinton-infected uranium bribery scandal and the prematurely drafted FBI memo to exonerate the most recently defeated United States presidential candidate, Hillary Clinton, who, by the way, is still acting like a heat-seeking missile in search of just one plausible excuse for her loss. Let's look at these scandals in turn.

The Obama administration was clearly spying on the Trump campaign during the presidential campaign, but was it based on good-faith evidence something untoward was occurring? Separate investigations are underway in both the Senate and the House to determine whether the administration relied on the so-called "Trump dossier" to obtain a Foreign Intelligence Surveillance Act warrant authorizing its "wiretapping" of Trump officials.

What's the problem with that, you ask? Well, you can't just throw things against the FISA wall to justify suspending Americans' privacy. The dossier is full of unsubstantiated information alleging elaborate connections between Trump and Russia — mouthwatering to Trump hunters but without calories.

The House Permanent Select Committee on Intelligence issued a subpoena to Fusion GPS, the opposition research company behind the dossier, which was authored by former British MI6 agent Christopher Steele. Fusion GPS' attorneys asserted "constitutional privileges" on behalf of the company's executives in refusing to deliver the subpoenaed documents. Swell.

The Daily Caller reports that Senate Judiciary Chairman Chuck Grassley raised several "alarming" questions in an Oct. 4 letter to FBI Director Christopher Wray. Did the FBI present dubious information from the dossier to the Foreign Intelligence Surveillance Court to obtain the warrant? If so, this would be a "staggering" revelation, according to former U.S. Attorney Joseph diGenova — "a type of manipulation of intelligence data and false intelligence data to mislead a court" that could require "the empanelment of a federal grand jury."

Grassley also asked whether Steele used the same information from the dossier in his report to British intelligence. Grassley is rightly concerned that the British report, though allegedly based on the same bogus information as the dossier, might have been fraudulently presented as independent corroboration of the dossier. So far, the FBI hasn't responded to three letters from Grassley seeking explanations for these anomalies.

Next, while the liberal media and the Democratic establishment shamelessly collude to find some scintilla of collusion between Trump and Russia to tamper with the presidential election, they've studiously avoided reporting on potentially real evidence of collusion between American officials and Russia. We've long heard allegations that the Clintons colluded with the Russians to enrich themselves at the expense of America's national security. But new evidence has emerged that may give this story some real teeth. The Hill's John Solomon and Alison Spann and Circa News reporter Sara Carter revealed that the FBI has acquired numerous documents, secret recordings, emails, financial records and eyewitness accounts allegedly proving that Russian nuclear officials caused millions of dollars to be paid to the Clinton Foundation and hundreds of thousands to be paid to Bill Clinton directly when Hillary Clinton was secretary of state. The State Department then approved the sale of 20 percent of America's uranium supply to Russia.

The Hill reports that the Obama administration was aware of these sordid transactions *before* it approved the deal to sell the uranium to the Russians in 2010: "The FBI had gathered substantial evidence that Russian nuclear officials were engaged in bribery, kickbacks, extortion and money laundering designed to grow Vladimir Putin's atomic energy business inside the United States, according to government documents and interviews." All kinds of other evidence was obtained showing Russian officials had "routed millions of dollars to the U.S. designed to benefit former President Bill Clinton's charitable foundation" while Hillary Clinton was secretary of state. But instead of bringing charges, the Obama Justice Department continued investigating — while the administration gave away our nuclear farm.

Even in the unlikely event that there is some less-than-incriminating explanation for all this, who can deny this is real collusion that resulted in dire consequences for our national security? Yet nary a peep elsewhere out of the liberal media. It seems they're only interested in false allegations of Russian collusion that involves Republicans — not in real collusion that involves the Democratic royal family, the Clintons.

Finally, for now, based on FBI documents, we know that former FBI Director James Comey began penning draft statements exonerating then-Democratic presidential candidate Hillary Clinton of criminal wrongdoing in the use of her personal email servers to host and transmit classified information before Comey had interviewed almost a dozen major witnesses, including Clinton herself. This is hardly a case of no harm, no foul, because in his announcement declining to bring charges, Comey declared that Clinton was guilty of egregious misconduct. He only declined to prosecute because he said the relevant criminal statute requires proof of criminal intent, which it manifestly does not and which exists anyway. Adding insult to injury, former U.S. Attorney General Eric Holder is publicly defending Comey's disgraceful act of prejudgment in favor of Hillary Clinton.

Liberals are frustrated that Donald Trump is in charge of their coveted executive branch and that their efforts to discredit, incriminate and impeach him for alleged Russian collusion are in free fall. Now they're pursuing plan B: Trump is too crazy to occupy the office. Democrats know a good offense is the best defense and the best diversion against evidence of Russian collusion — actual tangible proof of wrongdoing rather than partisan fabrication. Republicans need to pursue this reality as fervently as Democrats pursued their slanderous unreality.

There Is No GOP Civil War

October 27, 2017

Despite the unrequited longings of the left and certain vocal Republicans, there is no civil war in the Republican Party, and there is not even widespread disaffection with President Donald Trump among rank-and-file GOP voters.

But this is not what you would assume listening to Democrats and the mainstream media or frequenting the Twitter accounts of a number of high-profile Trump-disdaining conservatives.

Sen. John McCain has been in a public feud with President Trump, as have Sens. Bob Corker and Jeff Flake, who both have announced that they will retire, lamenting the decline in dignity and manners that Trump has allegedly ushered in. And no less a Republican well-wisher than Hillary Clinton has declared that the GOP is imploding.

President Trump, for his part, obviously perceives matters differently, tweeting, "The meeting with Republican Senators yesterday, outside of Flake and Corker, was a love fest." Even sometime Trump critic Lindsey Graham praised the luncheon, saying that Trump was "upbeat," "lighthearted" and "funny as hell."

With the liberal media gleefully showcasing these intramural squabbles and obsessing over Trump's every tweet and phone call, it's no wonder some might infer that Republicans are in hopeless disarray and headed for extinction. But outside their echo chamber and that of the denizens of NeverTrumpistan, I think we'll be fine.

Victor Davis Hanson, in a piece for National Review Online, cited data showing that despite perceptions to the contrary, Trump received roughly the same percentage of Republican votes as other previous GOP presidential candidates. Additionally, my own experience tells me that the overwhelming majority of fellow Republicans and conservatives are supportive of Trump, even if they don't wholeheartedly embrace everything he may tweet or say.

Indeed, very few conservatives I've run into are that concerned about Trump's tweets — even those who would prefer he dial them down a notch — because they appreciate that he is speaking their language instead of the guarded language of the typical politician. Columnist Salena Zito offered a fascinating insight on this, saying, "The press takes him literally, but not seriously; his supporters take him seriously, but not literally." Though certain conservative Trump critics cringe at this, I dare say the rank-and-file Republican voter understands the difference and isn't sweating the small stuff — provided we can move forward on policy and dismantle the Obama agenda.

Trump supporters don't dispute that Trump's bombastic style provides fodder for his critics, but they also understand that the political left has mercilessly savaged every other Republican president for decades. They believe that Trump is the first one, at least since Ronald Reagan, who gives the left a taste of its own medicine. This may be cringe-worthy to the Emily Posts of the conservative chattering class, but many of the rest of us are willing to overlook some of the distasteful in exchange for someone in our corner fighting back.

This is not to say that the Republican Party enjoys the greatest reputation these days, but that's more the fault of the recalcitrant moderates and the establishment wing than it is of Trump. Trump's most ardent conservative critics are the very ones who contributed to his rise in the first place — partly because they didn't perceive Obama's agenda as urgently destructive or they weren't willing to oppose him vigorously enough. And let's never underestimate the level of angst generated by the open-border advocates on the right who besmirched good-faith immigration hawks as nativists and racists. It's also hard to take seriously some (and I truly mean some, not all) never-Trumpers' insistence that they are the true conservatives when you often see them obsessing over Trump and you rarely see them criticizing the left; in fact, they frequently retweet liberals with approval.

What these critics don't grasp is that the Trump movement transcends Trump. It preceded him and will survive him. This does not necessarily mean in my view that populism will replace constitutional conservatism. But it does mean that rank-and-file conservatives are tired of their politicians talking a good game during their campaigns and losing their nerve in office and will now hold their candidates accountable.

As most recognize, Trump is not primarily ideological, though he does have a set of strong ideas on certain policies. I disagree with his protectionist bent, and I don't believe he should cater to the class warriors in promoting his otherwise attractive tax proposal. I also believe he could have been much more successful on Obamacare reform if he'd have tried to placate the bleeding hearts less via pre-existing conditions and mandated coverage and implement truly constructive market solutions.

But I am not fretting those differences. I am trying to speak up about them and hoping in my small way to influence the movement in a conservative direction.

Precisely because Trump is not a rigid ideologue, the policies of the so-called Trump movement — with certain exceptions, such as immigration — are not set in stone. Even on foreign policy, Trump has not shown himself to be a pure isolationist as some feared. He's a strong nationalist and patriot, but so are most constitutional conservatives. In many areas, Trump is governing as a mainstream conservative.

So no, the GOP is not imploding; it is experiencing a realignment whose parameters have yet to be fully drawn, so let's quit panicking and be constructive forces to shape this movement into one that's conservative, dynamic and determined to fight the left with the same amount of energy it uses to fight us. If we do that, we have every reason to expect to hold on to our governing majority.

Let There Be Light

November 3, 2017

"Let There Be Light" is a fabulous movie that has taken the box office by storm and by surprise, opening in a modest 373 theaters and exploding to more than 650 in just its second week.

Congratulations to director Kevin Sorbo and co-writer Sam Sorbo (also the lead actors in the film), co-writer Dan Gordon, and executive producer Sean Hannity. Kudos for giving moviegoers a charming alternative to the standard fare offered in theaters today.

Conservative Christians have learned constructive lessons in their struggle to contribute to the modern media and Hollywood culture, which routinely mocks and impugns their values and faith.

For years, Christians have exhorted one another to do more than just grumble about this cultural assault. "We have to get involved, producing movies, art, literature and other programming content instead of acting like whining victims."

Many artists throughout the media and cultural spectrum have stepped up and delivered faith-based content, and appreciative consumers have purchased and enjoyed it, but a common criticism has emerged for much of this product.

The legitimate complaint is that Christian-friendly television shows and motion pictures are overtly preachy and hokey. They mean well, but instead of seamlessly inserting the message into their shows, they use it as a sledgehammer and hit viewers over the head with it — projecting a sense of desperation. It's as if they sense their ideas are promoted so infrequently that they have to be in your face with them to make up the deficit.

This approach is often counterproductive because it violates the accepted rule that a writer should "show, not tell." There's certainly nothing wrong with characters in Christian movies quoting Scripture passages, but they should know they risk restricting their audience if they're too pious and sanctimonious. There's a clientele for such movies, but the movies most likely won't reach as many of the "unchurched" or have as much influence on the secular culture.

Liberals have learned to be subtler in their art, interweaving their political and secular themes in well-made dramas, so that even some viewers repulsed by the political message will endure the soft indoctrination because the stories are otherwise entertaining.

Some Christians and conservatives get it and are producing better-quality movies and incorporating their worldview inconspicuously into the content. There is a hunger among millions of Americans for the entertainment industry to provide content that at least doesn't disparage traditional values, even if it doesn't affirmatively promote them.

"Let There Be Light" admittedly hits Christian themes squarely, but it does so through authentic characters in normal settings whose experiences reflect those of everyday people in real life. It features humor and drama, but not fire and brimstone. The Christian characters are no less human than anyone else, nor are they immune from life's tribulations. Quite the opposite.

I first watched the movie in a screening at the National Religious Broadcasters convention in Orlando, and I've seen it several more times since and enjoyed it immensely each time.

Its characters display the full range of emotions — lows and highs, tears and laughter, despair and hope, raw anger and genuine joy, and deep personal suffering answered by enduring faith. The movie evokes these sentiments in the audience as it identifies with the struggles of the characters and shares their emotional and spiritual turbulence.

The film shows how life's painful events and circumstances can lead even people of faith to turn against God — to forsake and abandon him because they believe he first abandoned them. Loss of a loved one can destroy one's faith or strengthen it immeasurably, and we see both aspects here.

I was taken by how movingly the characters reflect heartfelt agony and how such despair reverberates throughout the lives of the entire family and inner circle of the aggrieved.

But though this brokenness can destroy everything in its path, it can also be the catalyst for the casting off of personal pride, the turning to God in repentance and the resulting redemption of the human spirit that only God can offer. In this process, we witness the power of prayer, the cleansing of forgiveness and the perfection of God's love.

Beyond these general themes, I don't want to include any spoilers, because you need to see the movie for yourself for maximum impact.

It is a delightful antidote for the negativity currently bombarding us in the culture, a powerful faith-builder for believers and a winsome apologetic for doubters.

I won't pressure you to watch this movie simply because we want to subsidize faith-based films. Movies should stand on their own merit — and this one does. No, don't go see this movie to support a cause or as a favor to the producers; see it as a favor to yourselves. You'll thoroughly enjoy it and profit from it.

Don't Mock Prayer. Pray

November 10, 2017

While the unspeakable massacre in a small church in Sutherland Springs, Texas, brought the best out of people there, it triggered the worst in certain others who see everything through their tainted political lenses.

House Speaker Paul Ryan tweeted: "Reports out of Texas are devastating. The people of Sutherland Springs need our prayers right now."

Leftist screamer Keith Olbermann responded, "Speaker Ryan, bluntly: shove your prayers up your a— AND DO SOMETHING WITH YOUR LIFE BESIDES PLATITUDES AND POWER GRABS."

It wasn't just Olbermann. Another God hater exclaimed: "They were in church. They had the prayers shot right out of them. Maybe try something else." Another said: "The murdered victims were in a church. If prayers did anything, they'd still be alive, you worthless sack of s—-."

Mass shootings invariably enrage militant gun control zealots at Second Amendment supporters, who they see as the repository of evil, and perhaps more responsible for these massacres than the gunmen themselves. I wish I were exaggerating.

Some of my favorite leftist Twitter stalkers ridiculed me for defending Ryan, expressing their contempt for Christians who call for prayer after these tragedies. When challenged, they insist they are mainly outraged that we won't take "real" action to stop the killings.

But we don't oppose reasonable restrictions designed to protect society from the evil and the insane — the kind that were already in place but not implemented in the case of the wife-abusing, God-hating perpetrator Devin Patrick Kelley.

Christians don't use prayer as an excuse for inaction. We don't believe our petitions to the Almighty relieve us of our duty to do good works. Christian theologian James Montgomery Boice said, "A strong prayer life is not the least bit inconsistent with vigorous and fervent service for the Lord. ... Prayer warriors are needed. But this does not mean that those who are active in Christian work (or any kind of work) do not also need to be strong in praying for God's direction and blessing."

Truth be told, the critics aren't wrestling with such philosophical questions, and they aren't calling for just any action. No. The only actions that will satisfy them are extreme gun control measures, which they wrongly believe will prevent these shootings.

In their anger, they lash out at prayer and God, mainly because they associate prayer with the type of person who blocks their gun-grabbing crusade.

Many have already answered their fallacious gun control arguments, so I want to briefly address their mocking of prayer.

In their tweets, you feel their rage at the God they deny exists. You sense their sneering hostility at the supposed futility of prayer, and their fury regarding their conceited assumption that Christians are only offering their "thoughts and prayers" to dodge the moral imperative of gun control.

Can they really misunderstand us that much? Do they think we believe we're off the hook if we throw up a few insincere sound bites to the God we actually believe in — and fear (revere and respect)? Heaven help us if that's what we're about.

So, why do we pray?

Why would we pray to an omniscient, sovereign God who knows our requests before we think them? Foremost, it's a matter of obedience. God commands us to pray without ceasing (1 Thessalonians 5:17; Colossians 4:2). Scripture tells us that God listens to our prayers (Psalm 139:1-4; 1 Kings 8:52) and responds to them. James 5:16 reads in part, "The prayer of a righteous person has great power as it is working." In fact, we'll fail to receive certain things simply by not asking for them (James 4:2).

Besides, prayer is not simply a one-way communication — a series of petitions to an omnipotent God with the expectation that He'll grant our wishes like a genie from a bottle. In prayer, we are conversing with the God of the universe to whom we have instant access. Yes, we ask God for things, but we also pray to express adoration to Him, to confess our sins, to seek His guidance, to praise Him and to give Him thanks.

But we can't expect that He will grant every request. Can you imagine the chaos that would ensue if billions of imperfect people were to have their contradictory prayers answered by an omniscient, omnipotent God? We should remember that we must pray in accordance with God's will — a will that we can't always perfectly discern.

Our triune God is relational and models His loving relationship for His church. Accordingly, Christians rightly believe that prayer strengthens the Christian community, and that with prayer there is power in numbers. Few things exhibit the spirit of Christ like congregations of believers lovingly praying for one another.

If you believe prayer is a pointless exercise, perhaps you'll sober up when you recall that Jesus Christ Himself, God Incarnate, continually prayed to the Father and directed us to do the same.

In fact, at the time of His greatest distress, before His imminent crucifixion, Jesus selflessly prayed for His people. One of the most moving passages of Scripture is the high priestly prayer related in John 17:1-26. In His spiritual agony, Jesus anticipated the Father's separation and wrath for his substitutionary sacrifice for mankind's sins; nevertheless, he pleaded with the Father for our joy, and for the Father to protect us from the evil one. He asked that we all be united as one, just as the Father and Son are united as one. "I in them and you in me, that they may become perfectly one."

Of course we must pray for those suffering among us. Only God knows precisely what they need. We are encouraged and mutually lifted up by one another's faith and prayers. As the Apostle Paul told the Romans, "I remember you in my prayers at all times ... that you and I may be mutually encouraged by each other's faith."

How about a little less pride and cynicism, and a little more faith and prayer as we confront these horrible human and societal evils?

Being Shoved Into Meaninglessness

November 17, 2017

I'm an advocate of higher education and all, but so much for assuming that the development of common sense and sound judgment are part of the package.

A Pew Research Center poll found that 77 percent of Democrats with a bachelor's degree or more believe a person's gender can be different from the sex they were "assigned at birth." You'll remember that Democrats are the party of science, and Republicans the Neanderthal science-deniers.

First we have to ask ourselves why in the world it would occur to anyone of any gender at any time or any place even to conduct such a survey. It would be like surveying people to find if they believe ears are for hearing or eyes for seeing.

It would be disturbing enough if only 77 percent of Democrats with this level of education thought gender is determined biologically. But 23 percent? That's a whole new level of weird — unless you define "weird" as being outside the mainstream. What's weird is how weird the mainstream has become — at least on the political left. This doesn't speak well for higher education in this country, does it? Then again, you wouldn't be surprised if you had seen the core curricula of America's "great" universities — and many of the required reading assignments in the classes.

I watched an interesting video of a young conservative from a liberal family explaining why he could dialogue with liberals and still love them because we all share common goals. It is leftists, he said, who don't even share our goals anymore, and it is very difficult to find any common ground with them.

I thought to myself when watching the video, "Yes, we do share some of the same goals: less crime, less poverty, etc., but increasingly the mainstream Democratic Party is embracing or strongly enabling certain extremist ideas. There is just no denying that the party has lurched leftward."

Reading these poll results, sadly, tends to validate my concerns, which is not something I'm happy about. How can a significant percentage of people of any respected group, much less of the higher-educated subset of that group, be so wrongheaded? People urging bipartisanship should explain how we find common ground with such stunningly different worldviews.

I'm hoping this chasm is partially due to the phrasing of the survey questions or fear of political correctness policing — but still, it's seriously problematic.

I don't doubt, by the way, that some very small fraction of a percentage of people sense they are trapped in their bodies and feel more like the opposite biological gender. I recently talked to such a person and am sure he was sincere. He has always felt like he should have been born a female. Note that he fully acknowledges, however, that he wasn't. He doesn't dispute the biological reality.

So I have no inclination to judge such people. If they feel opposite their biological gender, they do. It's above my pay-grade to fully understand this. But I think we're dealing with something more than this. Cultural activism is at work here.

Just look at the language the Pew survey uses to address these ideas: A human being's gender is "assigned at birth." You surely don't believe this language is accidental, do you?

To have an assignment there must be an assignor. If they mean God, or even nature, I'd have no quarrel, but it's clear they are talking about human agents (doctors or other health care providers) as assignors. This suggests some arbitrariness in the determination, or at least something that is subject to question.

It is not subject to question. Absent some biological aberration we are born either male or female, and no amount of linguistic manipulation can alter that reality, even though it obviously alters some people's perception of the reality.

Yes, there is certainly an agenda at work here; with the left everything is political. There is an effort to normalize that which is not normal, which introduces uncertainty into things certain. We have not evolved, but are being pushed headlong into moral relativism and further into post-modernism and beyond, where there is no such thing as truth and reality is just a function of the individual's preference.

This is moral chaos, intellectual chaos and biological chaos. It is nihilism. If truth is no longer defined as that which corresponds with reality, we have completely untethered ourselves from our foundations of meaning and significance. Parents with any remaining affinity for traditional values must surely be concerned about what we are bequeathing our children.

I'm not citing these ominous trends to score political points, and I acknowledge they are not solely the fault of just one political party, though they are disproportionately prevalent in that party. This is a societal and cultural problem that has polluted downstream political waters.

Indeed, these developments transcend politics. At the risk of subjecting myself to anti-Christian scoffing, I believe we are in the throes of spiritual warfare, which is one reason I'm not attempting to unduly demonize people falling prey to it. I used not to believe in the devil, but that was then, and this is now. I have no other rational explanation for morality and truth routinely being turned on their very heads — for right being considered wrong, and unreality masquerading as reality. Satan is the first and great deceiver, and many people, most of them unwittingly, are being deceived.

Pray for America. Pray for mankind.

Memo to GOP: Pass the Tax Bill

December 1, 2017

For a host of reasons, it is extremely important that Republicans pass the most pro-growth tax reform bill that can squeak by both houses of Congress.

Though President Trump's tweets and manners upset a lot of people, what seems to be lost in the mix is that his administration is making progress along many fronts. It's not just his judicial appointments, though it is difficult to overstate how excellent these have been.

He has also quietly made improvements in a number of other areas, scaling back oppressive administrative regulations on the environment, immigration and health care. The administrative state is a galloping cancer on our liberties that Congress rarely reins in, so Trump deserves credit for lawfully rescinding some of Barack Obama's unlawful orders.

Trump has also helped restore pride in America by promoting the American idea and expressing pride in and supporting the military and our national defense. He has not yet been the trade protectionist I feared, and he has been more circumspect in foreign policy than some anticipated.

But unless Trump is able to advance his legislative agenda, Republicans will be handicapped in 2018, not to mention 2020. Aware of this, Democrats will conspire to thwart any GOP tax bill, even one they would support if they were in charge.

Though the mouth-foaming left can't seem to discern this, Trump is not strongly ideological. Liberals see any Republican president as a right-wing extremist who must be stopped at all costs.

Trump's idiosyncratic behavior makes him all the more contemptible to them, but they would oppose his agenda just as fervently if he had pristine manners like, say, George W. Bush or Mitt Romney.

And though Trump's non-ideological bent may work to his advantage in some cases, it is clearly a detriment to advancing a legislative agenda. This is one place where governance is markedly different from running a business.

Though a handful of recalcitrant Republican senators can rightfully be blamed for the GOP's failure thus far to repeal Obamacare, Trump might very well have been able to overcome this obstacle had he presented a clearer vision. The problem is that he didn't have one and was too malleable, by which he forfeited his ability to build a coalition and lead on the issue. He just wanted a victory, and that is never enough.

The deeper problem was that he was of two minds on the issue. He was trying to reconcile conflicting goals — to reinstitute market forces in health care without removing the underlying socialistic structure of Obamacare.

We are seeing a bit of the same with the tax bill. The current bill is partially pro-growth, especially on the corporate side, but is schizophrenic because it incorporates the Democrats' class-warfare assumptions. I believe that Trump erred in allowing the Democrats to frame the debate in their terms when he said the rich don't need a tax cut — as if their money belongs to the government and they can only keep what the government, in its beneficence, allows.

Another major problem is that Republicans have tacitly conceded that every bill has to be "revenue-neutral" based on static scoring. That is, for every dollar in taxes they cut, they have to raise taxes somewhere else, totally factoring out the growth-generating aspects of reduced marginal rates. Republicans throw in part of the towel before negotiations begin.

Even if you believe that reducing tax rates won't expand the revenue pie, why is their default position to raise taxes elsewhere to pay for cuts instead of reducing spending?

I doubt that I will be ecstatic with whatever version finally emerges from Congress, but based on current proposals, I am optimistic that it will be a significant improvement over the status quo in substantially reducing corporate rates and individual rates on most of the middle class (the poor don't pay) and in simplifying the code.

I pray that the Republicans pass the best version they can so that they can fulfill one promise and then move on to spending issues and revisit health care reform — from a stronger position.

When they turn to spending, they will have to face the unpleasant reality that it is numerically impossible to curb the federal leviathan without once and for all tackling so-called entitlements. The Democrats will never do it, and they'll force Republicans to walk over hot coals in hell to make any progress here, but that's better than bequeathing our children fiscal hell.

I was encouraged to read recently that Paul Ryan and others in the GOP leadership fully intend to work on these issues next. If we think health care and taxes are a tough sell, just wait for entitlements.

So let's not allow, once again, the perfect to be the enemy of the good but encourage Congress to pass tax reform. The market is up based on positive signals, but those signals, as soon as possible, must be reinforced by real legislation. The clock is ticking.

Republican Trump Critics
Missing the Boat

December 8, 2017

I am probably too exercised over the never-Trump faction, because in the end, it's doubtful it is strong enough numerically to make a significant impact on our electoral politics, but it still bothers me to witness intramural conservative battles.

I have no quarrel with those who once self-identified as never-Trumpers but now appraise his actions and statements on a case-by-case basis instead of reflexively opposing his every move. My frustration is with those who obsess over Trump and lie in wait to pounce on any real or imagined Trump misstep like panting dogs drooling under the choice slab of beef hovering above them.

I don't want to paint with too broad a brush, but these are the types of conservatives whose tweets relentlessly savage Trump and harshly judge other conservatives who dare to support or defend him — on darn near anything. They mock and judge, judge and mock, preen and point, point and preen, forever lamenting the end of decency among many conservatives and the death of the Republican Party.

They excoriate conservatives for allegedly abandoning conservatism, painfully oblivious to their hypocrisy in often making their case on hyper-leftist shows with conservative-hating hosts and guests or fawningly retweeting leftists who have as much contempt for any conservative as they do for Donald Trump.

These critics argue that conservative Trump supporters have been tainted by their association with Trump, yet they jump in bed with those who haven't a stitch of conservatism in their entire anatomy. They're not just freely cohabiting foxholes with leftists; they are gradually drifting their way on policy.

They wouldn't be as annoying if they weren't so sanctimonious about their professed conservative purity and so judgmental about conservatives generally supportive of Trump, which brings me to what inspired this column.

A prominent Republican Trump critic with whom I'm friendly on Twitter betrays increasing dismay over the perceived betrayal of conservative Trump supporters. That we aren't alongside the naysayers lambasting Trump at every juncture, that we aren't mortified by every Trump tweet, is agonizingly disillusioning to him.

This week, he tweeted dolefully, "In the end, there will only be two groups of conservatives: those who sold out to Trumpism, and those who didn't. The policy differences among us pale next to that one major division."

Do you smell the judgmentalism — the rush to judge the motives of friends on the right? Note the language — we have "sold out to Trumpism," which is inarguably a sweeping moral condemnation of conservative Trump supporters.

It can't be that the countless millions of us believed — correctly — that Trump would be light-years better than Hillary Clinton as president or that, horrors, the critics were wrong. It can't be that we support Trump's major advancements in deregulation, his stellar judicial appointments and his efforts to cut taxes and repeal the abominable Obamacare individual mandate. It can't be his support of the military and national defense, his refreshing and contagious bullishness on America or his election alone, which stands as the greatest impediment to the further advancement of Obama-Clinton leftism. Oh, did I mention that Trump declared Jerusalem the official capital of Israel, as opposed to his presidential predecessors who merely paid lip service to the goal? And did you notice that the economy is smoking along at 3.3 percent growth?

In addition to their insufferable conceit, the critics are embarrassingly out of touch with and grossly underestimate rank-and-file conservatives, which is the most egregious consequence of their arrogance. The tens of millions of conservative Trump supporters numerically dwarf his hand-wringing critics — a reality that is inaccessible to them in their self-constructed bubble. They either don't realize how outnumbered they are or have contempt for the majority who don't share their narrow moralistic calculus. Millions of everyday American conservatives — even if they don't wholly approve of Trump's style, manners or idiosyncrasies — are cheering Trump on and grateful he has stopped the Democrats in their tracks and is moving the country back to the right.

So, as I've written before, I don't believe there is a serious schism in the grass-roots conservative movement. I don't believe that constitutional conservatives who are now supporting Trump have sold their souls or jettisoned their principles. They have not sold out; they have bought into the big picture.

I don't contend that Trump is a constitutional conservative, but he is advancing conservative policies more than any president in a long time — probably more than, say, Mitt Romney would have been able to. I don't agree that by supporting Trump, conservatives have ceded control of the party to an undefined populist movement — and certainly not to an alt-right cabal. If anything, Trump is moving more toward conservatism than conservatives are moving toward populism.

I have no animus for the malcontented Trump haters on the right and strive not to judge them — though I strongly disagree with them. But I sure wish they would quit judging the millions upon millions of the rest of us, whom they manifestly don't understand.

GOP Needn't Despair About Alabama

December 15, 2017

Republicans should not be disheartened by Roy Moore's loss in Alabama, because the election had little to do with Doug Jones — and probably even less with Donald Trump or the Republican agenda.

Don't get me wrong. It's quite troubling that the GOP's thin Senate majority just became anorexic, but this election by itself is not a predictor of a Democratic rout in 2018. Republicans could sustain substantial losses, to be sure, but the Alabama election doesn't make that foreseeable.

Roy Moore was a uniquely problematic candidate with more baggage than many Republicans believed they could excuse. Though it is remarkable that a Republican candidate lost in crimson-red Alabama, it is also noteworthy that even with his problems, he came close to winning.

The vast majority of Alabama Republicans did not want to sit home or to vote for Jones, because they understand the magnitude of the stakes before us. Yet enough of them did. Apparently, the fact that he would have doubtlessly voted as a conservative at a time when every single Republican vote is critical wasn't enough to overcome the sexual allegations and other concerns about Moore for these voters.

Also, America's political situation is particularly fluid, and there are too many variables and important events yet to play out for us to reliably forecast the 2018 election results. One savvy politician told me this week that he could see Republicans losing the majority in both houses in 2018 — but he also wouldn't be surprised if they were to actually gain seats if the economy remains strong and Trump's agenda continues apace.

Democrats have more Senate seats to defend in 2018 (26) than Republicans (eight), 10 of which are in states Trump carried in 2016 — five by double digits. Even CNN concedes that the electoral map "still clearly favors Republicans." But like other liberals, they are counting on Trump's supposed unpopularity and soaring passion in the Democratic base to offset any GOP advantages.

Moreover, prudent analysis has to factor in the adage that people vote with their pocketbooks — even young people, the demographic reputed to be least enamored with President Trump. A Bank of America/USA Today Better Money Habits survey conducted before the 2016 election showed that 65 percent of voters ages 18 to 26 would base their votes more on economic policies than on social issues.

Economic indicators are decidedly positive now, and notwithstanding Barack Obama's delusional post-presidential assertion that he deserves the credit for it, it's hard to dispute that Trump deserves the lion's share of credit.

The economy is humming well above 3 percent — a threshold the Obama malaise architects had already written off as no longer attainable. Unemployment is way down, and the stock market is surging significantly above impressive Obama-era levels.

This is real growth, as opposed to the fake growth Obama defeatists were touting when the economy was stagnating at 1 percent. And it can be traced to Trump's actions and the attitude he carried into office, just as Obama's stagnation can be traced to his business-hostile bearing.

Trump is bullish on America, the free market and American business. Entrepreneurs have responded accordingly, as have consumers. (Look at Christmas season sales already this year.) Trump has also been aggressive in rolling back stifling bureaucratic regulations across the board, and no one should underestimate the impact of his decision to back out of the Paris climate accord — or his support of the coal and natural gas industries.

Trump also tried, albeit unsuccessfully, to substantially revise, if not wholly repeal, Obamacare, and he is determined to try again. He and congressional Republicans have done a better job so far with the tax reform bill. Though it is imperfect and not the bill I would craft if I were king, it would meaningfully improve the existing law and is very close to being passed.

If it passes, I believe we'll see even more growth and far more revenues than the experts — the same ones who predicted that our days of 3 percent growth were over — are forecasting.

Yes, things could so south, especially if Trump and Congress are unable to move the tax bill and other major items of legislation before the 2018 elections, but I'm feeling upbeat.

My main concern is chaos within the Republican Party. The angst toward Trump among many Republicans is palpable, and unfortunately, a disproportionate number of these opponents are influential in the media.

I understand the naysayers' disapproval of Trump's style and various other complaints. But I don't understand why they won't acknowledge the positive developments that are occurring during his presidency — even if they have too much pride to give him credit for them. I get (and sometimes share) their distaste for his tweets, but it's baffling that they won't concede that on policy, at least, he has been far different from — and almost entirely better than — what they gloomily warned he would be.

He's not governing like a so-called populist nationalist, and he certainly hasn't advocated liberal policies as many feared. No matter what you think of Trump personally, he is advancing a largely conservative agenda.

Unlike some of Trump's perpetual critics, I don't worry that Trump is going to usher in an era of alt-right dystopia or that the country is going to descend into Bannonism — whatever that means. The critics shouldn't fear that Trump will forever taint the conservative movement or that America will descend into darkness.

America was descending into darkness under Obama's eight years, and that process would have accelerated into warp speed had Hillary Clinton been elected. So could we please lighten up and support the president when he's advancing salutary policies, which is often, and go into 2018 with a spirit of warranted optimism?

A Celebration of Life

December 22, 2017

People often lament that in our celebration of Christmas, we tend to lose sight of its true meaning. Not to be a contrarian, but I don't think the two are mutually exclusive.

At Christmastime, we celebrate family, giving, tradition, friendship, community, love, goodwill and so much else that is great and good about human existence. These sublime experiences and institutions are wonderful precisely because our savior, in whom goodness inheres, created them.

With proper godly perspective, delighting in these glorious gifts actually enhances our focus on God; it doesn't diminish it. Of course, we must discipline ourselves, if it doesn't occur naturally, to give thanks to God and to consciously savor him and his gift of life to us.

This time of year, we celebrate Christ's incarnation — his birth, his earthly example and his miracles and teachings. We humbly bow at the Crucifixion, marvel at the magisterial Resurrection and gratefully acknowledge our regeneration salvation in him. We cherish that he is truth, the judge and the very giver of life.

Unlike the mythical god of deism, our God did not create us and then callously abandon us to a desperate state of sinfulness, misery and suffering. He is not only the Creator but also the sustainer of the universe. The writer of Hebrews assures us, "He upholds the universe by the word of His power." The Apostle Paul proclaims, "He is before all things, and in Him all things hold together."

Though God gave us the freedom to sin and mankind subsequently fell, Christ became sin for us, thereby conquering sin and death. He offers us redemption and eternal life in his presence.

It is fitting that we celebrate Christ's birth, because his redeeming work on our behalf — his death on the Cross and thus our salvation — could not have been accomplished without his incarnation. It is all part of a piece. If he had merely been in form a human but in substance only God, his suffering, the Crucifixion and the Resurrection would have been illusory.

Paul wrote to the Philippians: "Have this mind among yourselves, which is yours in Christ Jesus, who, though he was in the form of God, did not count equality with God a thing to be grasped, but emptied himself, by taking the form of a servant, being born in the likeness of men. And being found in human form, he humbled himself by becoming obedient to the point of death, even death on a cross."

Jesus wasn't just the greatest of all human prophets. He was fully God and fully man, a truth that Christians believed from the beginning and that the Council of Chalcedon formally affirmed in A.D. 451. "Therefore, following the holy fathers, we all with one accord teach men to acknowledge one and the same Son, our Lord Jesus Christ, at once complete in Godhead and complete in manhood, truly God and truly man, consisting also of a reasonable soul and body; of one substance with the Father as regards His Godhead, and at the same time of one substance with us as regards His manhood."

Christianity's critics sometimes question God's permitting human suffering, but the Cross, to paraphrase the late Pastor John Stott, smashes those concerns to smithereens. Christ understands our suffering and even our mundane problems because he became one of us and experienced what we experience. "For we do not have a high priest who is unable to sympathize with our weaknesses, but one who in every respect has been tempted as we are, yet without sin" (Hebrews 4:15).

Christ suffered — so that we can live — more pain than anyone who has ever existed. It was not only his physical beatings and passion but also his excruciating separation from the Father and his endurance of God's wrath for all of the past, present and future sins of mankind. Moreover, God created us knowing at the time that Christ's human birth and sacrificial death would be necessary. John tells us that Jesus is "the Lamb that was slain from the creation of the world." A greater act of love is inconceivable.

Having become human and suffering as a human being, Christ is an empathetic, personal God, who is approachable to us and with whom we can have a personal relationship. "Let us then with confidence draw near to the throne of grace, that we may receive mercy and find grace to help in the time of need" (Hebrews 4:16).

This Christmas, let's celebrate the wonders of our existence as human beings created in God's image and with the capacity for his love, which we must abundantly share with one another. Let's draw near to his throne of grace, profusely thanking him for the undeserved mercy he gave us and meditating on "whatever is true, whatever is honorable, whatever is just, whatever is pure, whatever is lovely, whatever is commendable" (Philippians 4:8).

About the Author

David Limbaugh is a lawyer, a nationally syndicated columnist, a conservative political commentator and the author of eight New York Times best-sellers: "The True Jesus," "The Emmaus Code," "Jesus on Trial," "The Great Destroyer," "Crimes Against Liberty," "Bankrupt," "Persecution" and "Absolute Power."

As an expert in law and politics, Limbaugh has appeared on hundreds of national and local television and radio shows, including Fox News Channel's "Hannity," "Fox & Friends" and "Your World with Neil Cavuto," CNN's "Crossfire" and "The Situation Room with Wolf Blitzer," CNBC's "The Kudlow Report" and CBN's "NewsWatch," as well as "The Sean Hannity Show," "The Mark Levin Show," "The Laura Ingraham Show," "The Mike Gallagher Show," "The Michael Medved Show," "The Dennis Miller Show" and "The Dennis Prager Show."

Limbaugh has been practicing law for almost 40 years and currently specializes in entertainment and contract law. He graduated cum laude from the University of Missouri and received his law degree from the University of Missouri School of Law. He was a member of the Missouri Law Review and also served in the National Guard.

The brother of radio talk show host Rush Limbaugh, David Limbaugh lives in Cape Girardeau, Missouri, with his wife and children.

THE LEFT JUST ISN'T RIGHT
is also available as an e-book
for Kindle, Amazon Fire, iPad, Nook and
Android e-readers. Visit
creatorspublishing.com to learn more.

○ ○ ○

CREATORS PUBLISHING

We publish books.
We find compelling storytellers and
help them craft their narrative,
distributing their novels and collections
worldwide.

○ ○ ○

Made in the USA
Lexington, KY
18 November 2018